D1361436

Fingerprints and Impression Evidence

Other titles in the Crime Scene Investigations series:

Fingerprints and Impression Evidence

by Jenny MacKay

LUCENT BOOKS

An imprint of Thomson Gale, a part of The Thomson Corporation

THOMSON

GALE

Detroit • New York • San Francisco • New Haven, Conn. • Waterville, Maine • London

For more information, contact
Lucent Books
27500 Drake Rd.
Farmington Hills, MI 48331-3535
Or you can visit our Internet site at http://www.gale.com

LIBRARY OF CONGRESS CATALOGING-IN-PUBLICATION DATA

MacKay, Jenny, 1978-
Fingerprints and impression evidence / by Jenny MacKay.
  p. cm. — (Crime scene investigations)
Includes bibliographical references and index.
ISBN 978-1-4205-0037-0 (hardcover)
1. Fingerprints—Juvenile literature. 2. Criminal investigation—Juvenile literature. I. Title.
HV6074.M33 2008
363.25'8—dc22

2007040335

ISBN-10: 1-4205-0037-6
Printed in the United States of America

Contents

Foreword

The popularity of crime scene and investigative crime shows on television has come as a surprise to many who work in the field. The main surprise is the concept that crime scene analysts are the true crime solvers, when in truth, it takes dozens of people, doing many different jobs, to solve a crime. Often, the crime scene analyst's contribution is a small one. One Minnesota forensic scientist says that the public "has gotten the wrong idea. Because I work in a lab similar to the ones on *CSI*, people seem to think I'm solving crimes left and right—just me and my microscope. They don't believe me when I tell them that it's just the investigators that are solving crimes, not me."

Crime scene analysts do have an important role to play, however. Science has rapidly added a whole new dimension to gathering and assessing evidence. Modern crime labs can match a hair of a murder suspect to one found on a murder victim, for example, or recover a latent fingerprint from a threatening letter, or use a powerful microscope to match tool marks made during the wiring of an explosive device to a tool in a suspect's possession.

Probably the most exciting of the forensic scientist's tools is DNA analysis. DNA can be found in just one drop of blood, a dribble of saliva on a toothbrush, or even the residue from a fingerprint. Some DNA analysis techniques enable scientists to tell with certainty, for example, whether a drop of blood on a suspect's shirt is that of a murder victim.

While these exciting techniques are now an essential part of many investigations, they cannot solve crimes alone. "DNA doesn't come with a name and address on it," says the Minnesota forensic scientist. "It's great if you have someone in custody to match the sample to, but otherwise, it doesn't help.

That's the investigator's job. We can have all the great DNA evidence in the world, and without a suspect, it will just sit on a shelf. We've all seen cases with very little forensic evidence get solved by the resourcefulness of a detective."

While forensic specialists get the most media attention today, the work of detectives still forms the core of most criminal investigations. Their job, in many ways, has changed little over the years. Most cases are still solved through the persistence and determination of a criminal detective whose work may be anything but glamorous. Many cases require routine, even mind-numbing tasks. After the July 2005 bombings in London, for example, police officers sat in front of video players watching thousands of hours of closed-circuit television tape from security cameras throughout the city, and as a result were able to get the first images of the bombers.

The Lucent Books Crime Scene Investigations series explores the variety of ways crimes are solved. Titles cover particular crimes such as murder, specific cases such as the killing of three civil rights workers in Mississippi, or the role specialists such as medical examiners play in solving crimes. Each title in the series demonstrates the ways a crime may be solved, from the various applications of forensic science and technology to the reasoning of investigators. Sidebars examine both the limits and possibilities of the new technologies and present crime statistics, career information, and step-by-step explanations of scientific and legal processes.

The Crime Scene Investigations series strives to be both informative and realistic about how members of law enforcement—criminal investigators, forensic scientists, and others—solve crimes, for it is essential that student researchers understand that crime solving is rarely quick or easy. Many factors—from a detective's dogged pursuit of one tenuous lead to a suspect's careless mistakes to sheer luck to complex calculations computed in the lab—are all part of crime solving today.

A Criminal's Touch

In the town of Corey, Pennsylvania, the wife of a bank manager was kidnapped for ransom, and during the ordeal, she was murdered. The kidnapper had made a rough draft of his ransom note before typing the real thing. He ripped this draft into fifteen small squares and threw it in a garbage can behind the store that he owned. Police later found the torn pieces of paper, and when they were processed, the kidnapper's fingerprints were found on eight of them. "He claimed that it was paper from his store and someone else took the blank paper and typed the note," said Gary W. Jones, a former supervisory fingerprint specialist for the Federal Bureau of Investigation (FBI), as he described the case.

> I noted that his fingerprints were in the center area of each of the eight torn pieces. It would have been impossible for someone else to tear the note around each one of his fingerprints before they were developed. I was able to testify that not only were the latent [hidden or difficult to see] fingerprints his, but he also was the one who tore the note.[1]

Criminals may lie, but impression evidence does not. For many years, crooks have been betrayed by the markings they leave behind at the scene of a crime. A muddy footprint, a tire track, or a mark from a crowbar could be the clue that investigators need to link a crime to the person who committed it. But the most compelling impression evidence is often invisible. It takes the form of tiny lines and swirls left behind in sweat by human skin. Finding these clues from fingers, palms, feet, and toes is the job of a fingerprint specialist. For more than a century, fingerprint experts have chased down criminals using only the patterns of the lines on the criminal's feet and hands. The tiny ridges of this "friction skin" are so unique to their owners that no two fingerprints (or, palm or foot prints) have ever been found to be identical.

If a fingerprint is found at a crime scene and it belongs to a suspect who had no honest reason to be there, it may be all the evidence investigators need to prove the person's guilt in a courtroom. Crime scene investigators put a great deal of time and energy into finding, developing, and preserving finger-prints. It is dirty and painstaking work. Fingerprint experts often find themselves crawling under furniture or chopping out sections of walls to find and preserve the prints they are looking for.

Although a fingerprint expert's work is often painstaking and dirty, it is important since a fingerprint may be the only evidence linking a suspect to a crime scene.

They must also be clever, much like the criminals whose prints they are trying to find. They choose from dozens of methods to make fingerprints visible—specialized light sources, powders, and chemicals—and can find and develop prints on an increasing number of surfaces with every passing year.

In the early days of fingerprinting science, the note-tearing kidnapper described earlier may well have gone free. Investigators had to find fingerprints on the first draft of the ransom note without destroying the paper, which itself was important evidence. The ability to do this is a fairly recent development in fingerprint science. Experts are constantly looking for new and better ways to lift fingerprints and other suspicious impressions from difficult surfaces like these. It is now possible to get prints from paper, latex gloves, fabric, plastic bags, and perhaps even human skin.

In recent years, computer technology has greatly improved the way the FBI stores and searches for prints. A handful of likely matches for a crime scene print can be pulled from a database of millions in less time than it takes an investigator to break for coffee. This makes it possible for police officers to pinpoint people who have committed crimes and arrest them before they can strike again.

New fingerprints are always being added to the FBI's automated database. Every time a person gets arrested, applies for a job in the public-service sector, or joins the military, for example, their fingerprints are taken and entered into the database, where they will permanently remain on record. A large number of fingerprints in the FBI's database belong to honest and caring citizens such as teachers and social workers who have never broken any law. But the FBI's fingerprint identification system depends on recording and filing the prints of as many citizens as possible. The more fingerprint records the FBI keeps, the better the odds that a print left at a crime scene will lead investigators to a suspect or that an unidentified body may be matched with a name.

Impression evidence has been part of crime solving for so long that some people have come to think of it as run-of-the mill police work. In reality, finding these tiny and important clues takes a combination of luck, hard work, patience, a strong understanding of science, and cleverness on the part of the investigator. An untrained eye could find some of the impression evidence left at a crime scene, but an experienced crime scene veteran knows that the most important clues are often invisible. They must be coaxed out of hiding, with the most cutting-edge forensic techniques science can offer, and used to track down the unlawful people who unintentionally left them behind.

Experts in the field of impression evidence know that for a crime to be committed, a criminal must have touched something, moved something, or walked on something. A footprint, a fingerprint, a smudge from a glove—at every crime scene, there will be some kind of impression evidence. Crime scene specialists look for it, preserve it, and use it to track down the criminals who stamped some small trace of themselves on the scene of their crime. Any imprint, even an invisible one, brings investigators one step closer to solving the case.

CHAPTER 1

Identity by Fingers

No matter how much evidence is collected or how many experts are called in, solving a crime always boils down to one simple question—who did it? Investigators look for evidence that links one suspect more than others. But the best evidence is the kind that proves guilt beyond any doubt. It points to one suspect while excluding not just every other suspect, but every other person on Earth. The types of evidence that fall into this category are rare, but one of them has been part of forensic science for so long that it is hard to imagine forensics without it: the fingerprint.

All human beings have fingerprints. From birth to death, a person's fingerprints never change. And no two prints from any two fingers have ever been found to be exactly the same.

Members of the same family, and in fact, even identical twins have completely different fingerprints. A study of the fingerprint patterns of four generations of a single family found that none of the fingerprints of those family members resembled one another at all. Based on the results of this study, family genes have no effect on the way fingerprints will turn out.

"There were no similarities between any two fingers or any one member of this group or between any finger of one member to a finger of another member," said the study's author, Gaye Shahan.[2]

The absolute uniqueness of fingerprints makes them incredibly useful for criminal investigations. A fingerprint found at a crime scene can belong to one and only one person in the entire world. If the crime scene print can be matched to one individual, the police have a solid case.

The individuality of fingerprints, however, is purely a consequence of their true purpose.

An Uncivil Murder

The night civil rights activist Martin Luther King, Jr., was assassinated in Memphis, Tennessee, a rifle was found close to the Lorraine Motel where the murder took place. Fingerprints found on the rifle, the rifle's scope, and a nearby pair of binoculars matched those of an escaped convict named James Earl Ray. The fingerprint evidence helped lead police to the identification of Ray as their chief suspect. When they tracked him down in a London airport and arrested him, he realized the strength of the evidence against him and pled guilty to King's assassination. Ray was sentenced to ninety-nine years in prison.

James Earl Ray was convicted of killing Martin Luther King, Jr. based on the fact that his fingerprints were found on the rifle, the rifle's scope, and binoculars found at the scene.

The Structure of a Fingerprint

Skin is the largest organ in the human body, and it does many jobs. It protects and holds together the organs beneath it, keeps in moisture, acts as a barrier against germs, and helps to keep the body warm. Skin on some areas of the body has particular functions. Skin on the tongue, for example, is full of taste buds. Skin on the scalp has glands that release oils to keep the hair healthy. Other areas of skin are designed to hold onto things. The skin that we use for gripping is called friction skin. It is found on the palms of the hands, the soles of the feet, the bottoms of the toes, and the fingertips. Small ridges in friction skin work like the treads of a tire to create resistance. We call these papillary ridges. They make it easier to walk on a smooth surface without slipping, to climb a rope, or to hold a pencil.

Papillary ridges serve the same purpose in every human being, but they take on a wide variety of forms. Ridges might swirl or arch, or tent or loop. The directions these patterns take and the distances between the ridges are unique to any one area of friction skin. The patterns of papillary ridges differ not just from person to person, but even from finger to finger on the same hand. Any area of friction skin the size of a dime will be

A close-up of the ridges on a finger. The patterns of papillary ridges not only differ from person to person, but also from finger to finger on the same hand.

different than any other area of friction skin on that person's body or anyone else in the world.

Friction skin is also designed to sweat. Every square inch on the surfaces of the hands or feet contains around three thousand sweat glands. For the same reason that licking a finger helps

Are Television Crime Shows Realistic?

The experts weigh in:

"By far, the most common misperception (aided by programs like *CSI*) is that latent fingerprints are always left when a person touches something. That is not true. It is very difficult and just plain dirty work to develop latent prints. We are very fortunate to develop one. Also, crime scene technicians and fingerprint examiners look nothing like those on TV, where all the females wear five-inch heels and Donna Karen outfits and all the guys look like Brad Pitt."

—Gary W. Jones, former supervisory fingerprint specialist for the FBI

"Popular TV culture always lets the viewer know that the villain must wear gloves while committing the crime to avoid detection by the investigator. While this is great for TV, in real life, suspects do not always follow the teachings of their favorite TV show. Let's also not forget that there could be a hole in the glove."

—Graham Ford, fingerprint expert

"The CSI shows are fictional and unrealistic. The producers will even tell you that. But I don't know if we're making a smarter criminal with all these TV shows."

—Allyn DiMeo, forensic specialist

to turn a page in a book, the thin layer of sweat that is left behind on the surfaces we touch helps friction skin to grasp and hold onto things. In his book *Fingerprints: The Origins of Crime Detection and the Murder Case That Launched Forensic Science*, author Colin Beavan says these sweat glands make each finger "like a self-inking rubber stamp, leaving calling cards on every surface it touches."[3]

Because of their friction skin, people leave behind a trail of sweaty fingerprints wherever they go. This fact is the basis of dactyloscopy, the science of studying fingerprints for identification.

A Lifelong Marker

Early dactyloscopers were not trying to solve any crimes. They were just fascinated by the swirls on their own fingertips and were curious to see if anyone else's looked the same. Their early studies revealed that fingerprints seemed to be unique to every individual, but they also seemed to keep the same pattern from birth throughout life.

Modern science has shown that babies are born with a full set of unique and personalized fingerprints. In fact, distinctive patterns of friction skin develop in an unborn child as early as the third or fourth month of pregnancy.

The exact position of the fetus in the womb at a particular moment and the exact composition and density of surrounding amniotic fluid decides how every individual ridge will form," says Tom Harris, a contributing author for the website www.HowStuffWorks.com. "The entire development process is so chaotic that, in the entire course of human history, there is virtually no chance of the same exact pattern forming twice."[4]

The patterns a person has at birth are his or hers for life. They grow as the fingers grow, just as the design on a printed balloon grows as the balloon is inflated. The shape of the friction ridges and the relative distance between them, however,

A fetus in the womb. Scientists have discovered that fetuses develop a full set of unique fingerprints while in the womb.

stays the same. This means a specialist can match a grown man's prints to the tiny impressions that may have been taken shortly after his birth.

"The size of the print, which changes as we grow from infants to adults, is immaterial," says N. E. Genge, author of *The Forensic Casebook: The Science of Crime Scene Investigation.* He notes that distances between the various features of a fingerprint—where the papillary ridges meet, split apart, swirl, and form other patterns—are measured print by print, not according to a particular scale. "A dot might be found twice as far from a particular ridge as an island," Genge says. "That relationship of two to one doesn't change, regardless of how big the print becomes over time."[5]

Even in death, the patterns remain. If a corpse is found that cannot be identified by other means, forensic scientists are often able to take fingerprints and use them to identify the body. In fact, fingerprinting is now a common step performed during autopsies (post-mortem examinations) although slightly decomposed fingers may have to be reconstructed or even removed to complete the process.

Friction skin patterns are permanent, and they are also surprisingly stubborn. Papillary ridges can be scorched, sliced, scrubbed, sanded, blistered, or peeled off, and still, they will grow back in exactly the same patterns as before. Even a wart only changes the patterns temporarily. Papillary ridges will surround the wart, and once the wart is gone, the familiar patterns will be back again.

The permanence of fingerprints is one of the qualities that make them so useful for solving crimes, especially crimes committed by repeat offenders.

By the Numbers

1 IN 6 BILLION

Odds that two different people on earth will have an identical fingerprint pattern

A burglar may rob a bank at age eighteen and a grocery store when he is eighty, and the fingerprints he leaves at both scenes will match exactly. Serial criminals whose crimes continued for decades before their capture have been successfully linked to every scene where their fingerprints were found. In fact, it was the appeal of capturing serial criminals that encouraged early ideas of the use of fingerprints in detective work.

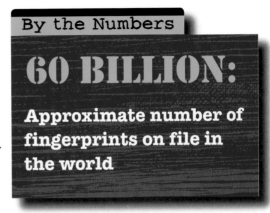

By the Numbers

60 BILLION:

Approximate number of fingerprints on file in the world

Signature Prints

In modern times, we take it for granted that fingerprints are used to catch crooks. This method was not always obvious, however. It was centuries before anyone connected the innocent-looking swirls on our fingers to their crime-solving potential. Instead, fingerprints were first used as a form of written signature. As early as 600 A.D., the Chinese and Japanese discovered how unique their own fingers were. They began stamping their fingerprints on everything from artwork to contracts in order to mark items as belonging to them. Many centuries later, in 1878, a Scottish missionary named Henry Faulds found examples of these signature fingerprints pressed into ancient Japanese pottery. It occurred to Faulds that if fingerprints could be a reliable way to brand the masterpiece of a particular artist, they might also be able to mark the handiwork of a criminal.

Faulds was not alone in thinking that fingerprints could be the next big thing in solving crime. At about the same time as he discovered the pottery prints, British colonial officers in India realized they could use finger and palm prints to identify colonists who could not write their own signature. One of these colonial officers, Sir Edward Richard Henry, developed a system for identifying different hand and palm prints. In 1901, Henry joined Scotland Yard, London's police headquarters. This gave him a chance to try out his fingerprinting theories in a new and exciting field of science—criminal investigation.

Sir Edward Richard Henry, police commissioner of Scotland Yard, was one of the first people to develop a system for identifying fingerprints found during a criminal investigation.

The early fingerprinting techniques used by Henry and his co-workers were quite different from those used today. Investigators were limited to collecting only the most obvious of fingerprints, such as those left in ink, and the science of fingerprinting was so new that often it was not taken seriously. There were few standard procedures for taking the fingerprints of convicted criminals, and there were even fewer techniques for preserving and clarifying the fingerprints found at crime scenes.

However, the idea of a foolproof method for linking criminals to crime scene evidence was too important to ignore. Early defenders of the fingerprinting system stubbornly kept trying to find and examine this new type of clue, to prove the value of using fingerprints.

A major breakthrough came in 1905 when police in Deptford, UK, arrived at the scene of a gory double murder. An elderly paint shop manager and his wife had been found beaten to death in their south-east London home. A sweep of the scene turned up a single bloody fingerprint that had been left on an empty metal cash box. The print did not match those of the murder victims or any officer at the scene. However, when two brothers, Albert and Alfred Stratton, were arrested as suspects and fingerprinted, Alfred's right thumbprint matched the cash-box print exactly. In one of the first murder cases to use fingerprint evidence in court, the Stratton brothers were convicted and sentenced to death by hanging. For the first time, a jury decided that fingerprint evidence was convincing enough to justify the death penalty.

Tracking Criminals

Although the case of the Stratton brothers was successful in court, it showed a weakness in the fingerprinting system. Fingerprints collected from crime scenes were only useful when there was a suspect's finger to compare them to. In such cases, fingerprints could prove guilt or innocence (which was just as important to the wrongly accused). But a central question

During the early 1900s, it was common practice for Scotland Yard police officers to spend long hours examining fingerprint files in order to try and match them to those found at a crime scene.

remained: could fingerprints be used to reveal the identity of an unknown suspect?

For fingerprints to be useful in this way, investigators needed a vast bank of fingerprints on file from a great many individuals. They also needed a reliable system for sorting these fingerprints so that a print left at a crime scene could be quickly compared to those on file. Without computers and other modern technology, this was an enormous task. It was also not helpful that the fingerprints that *were* kept on file were not always a full set of ten fingers.

By the early 1900s, it was standard procedure for British police officers to fingerprint criminals and keep their prints for

future reference. The officers felt that this would help them to identify which crooks had been arrested before. Recognizing repeat criminals rather than first-time offenders was clearly helpful when deciding on a fitting punishment; matching the prints of a known serial offender would help justify a harsher sentence. But when investigators had to work backward through fingerprint files, searching through thousands of records to find a match for a print, certain flaws in the system became painfully obvious.

One such case occurred when Leonardo da Vinci's painting the *Mona Lisa* was stolen from the Louvre, a Paris art museum, in 1911. The glass that had guarded the painting bore one clear fingerprint. Investigators spent several tiresome months sorting through thousands of fingerprint cards, but they did not find a match in their collection. Two years later, the thief was finally arrested, and the investigators were frustrated to discover that his prints and identity had been on file the whole time—they had taken only his right-hand fingerprints, but his left thumbprint had been left on the glass.

Improving the System

Cases such as this made it clear that the fingerprinting system needed improvement. First, detectives realized it was important to take fingerprints in a thorough and standard way. Recording the prints from all ten fingers of every suspect, and doing so in a specific sequence, would help to avoid a repeat of the *Mona Lisa* difficulties.

Second, fingerprint collections had to be improved and organized so they could be searched quickly and correctly for a particular match. The number of fingerprints kept on file continued to grow, making it more and more time consuming to search through the records one by one. A good system for sorting fingerprints would allow them, once filed away, to be easily found again, like dictionary entries classified by letter.

The classification system used in the early years of fingerprinting, and the one still used today, was the same as that designed by fingerprinting pioneer Sir Edward Richard Henry during his work in India. Henry's system sorts fingerprints by their general features: loops are filed with other loops, whorls with other whorls, and so on. To find a match for any crime scene print, investigators can ignore a large number of the prints on file and focus only on a few fingerprints that all have similar characteristics.

These improvements resulted in standardized files of fingerprints that could be easily searched. The new system was popular because it brought faster and more dependable methods of fingerprint identification. By the first decade of the 1900s, British police officers were enjoying one of the smartest inventions in the history of fighting crime.

Spreading the Word

The science of fingerprinting was considered such an important discovery that British police officers wanted to share the news with the rest of the world. They also realized that for fingerprint science to reach its full potential, it needed to be used internationally. Local fingerprint files were useful for catching local criminals, but offenders would become anonymous again if they moved to a different city where their fingerprints were not on file.

Eager to spread their fingerprinting knowledge with other countries, British experts crossed the Atlantic Ocean to the United States, where they found a ready audience for their science: the Federal Bureau of Investigation (FBI).

Fingerprinting technology came to North America during the 1904 World's Fair in St. Louis, Missouri. John Kenneth Ferrier, of the fingerprint branch of Scotland Yard, tutored St. Louis police officers on the basics of the fingerprinting technique. St. Louis became the first U.S. city to use fingerprinting to fight crime. Four years later, the FBI adopted the technology, and by the 1920s, it had established its own fingerprint bureau. By 1933, the FBI ironed out some of the fingerprinting problems that troubled Scotland Yard.

It perfected its own fingerprint system by creating a single-fingerprint file. Rather than classifying a known criminal's prints based on all ten fingers together, each of a criminal's ten prints could be sorted just by its own characteristics. Finding a match no longer depended on having all ten fingerprints present on the card in the file. Fingerprint matching was faster and easier than ever before.

In the 1970s, during the early days of computers, the FBI's fingerprinting bureau reached another milestone. It successfully created an automated fingerprint identification system, or AFIS, which used computers to scan, store, and search huge numbers of fingerprint files. It became possible to store vast amounts of fingerprint records in one location and to quickly search for a fingerprint among millions of stored entries. Criminals could no longer hide from their fingerprint records

A demonstration of an automated fingerprint identification system, or AFIS, in Concord, New Hampshire. AFIS makes it possible for the FBI to store and search vast amounts of fingerprint records in one location.

by moving to a different town; a fingerprint left at any crime scene in the country could be compared to the prints in the central, computerized system.

Gone, too, were the days of sifting through stacks of fingerprint cards by hand. Fingerprint specialists, now freed from this time-consuming task, could turn their attention to developing new ways of finding and preserving their evidence at crime scenes. Fingerprints and the experts who examined them rose to a new level of status in the science of fighting crime.

Why Fingerprints?

Of all the forensic tools in the hands of crime scene investigators, fingerprints are among the oldest. Impressive new technology such as DNA analysis might seem to outdate such an aging technique, but fingerprint evidence is still one of the most popular methods in crime scene investigation.

One reason is that fingerprints leave little room for argument. If prints are found at a crime scene, they were clearly left by the person who owns them. "They're the sort of evidence every detective wants to have in hand when a case goes to trial," says Genge. "No wonder fingerprints are major exhibits in so many trials."[6]

Fingerprints are also one of the most plentiful types of evidence left behind at a crime scene. DNA evidence from blood and other bodily fluids may be fairly common at scenes of violent crimes such as murder and rape, but it is rarely found where a nonviolent crime has been committed. However, any crime scene is likely to contain fingerprints that can lead investigators straight to the criminal.

"What is surprising," Genge says, "is how often criminals obligingly leave a print behind."[7]

Another strength of fingerprint evidence is that it carries weight in a criminal trial. Fingerprints have been a tool of law enforcement for so long that juries see them as reliable, easily understood evidence. "Aside from a few cases early in this century when the technique was new and familiar, there

are no recorded cases of juries choosing to ignore fingerprint evidence," says Simon Cole in his book *Suspect Identities: A History of Fingerprinting and Criminal Identification.* "Juries have convicted—and appeals courts have upheld those convictions—even when a latent fingerprint stood as the only evidence against a defendant."[8]

After three trials and thirty years, it was fingerprint evidence that finally convicted Byron de la Beckwith (pictured, center) for the 1963 murder of civil rights activist Medgar Evers.

An example of such a scenario was the trial of Byron de la Beckwith, a member of the Ku Klux Klan. De la Beckwith left his fingerprints on the rifle that police believed was used in the 1963 murder of Medgar Evers, a field secretary for the National Association for the Advancement of Colored People (NAACP). Two trials ended in 1964 with hung juries, and de la Beckwith went free. But when he was tried yet again thirty years later at the age of seventy-three, the fingerprint evidence was enough for the modern jury to finally convict him. He was sentenced to spend the rest of his life in prison.

Given the importance of a good, clear fingerprint, crime scene investigators do their best to ensure that not a single print goes undiscovered. The concept of fingerprint evidence is simple, but finding it remains a constant challenge. Looking for bloody imprints on metal cash boxes may have been good enough a century ago, but today's forensic scientists rely on a great deal more than luck. They must use every chemical and technological advance at their disposal to uncover these often hidden criminal markers and bring to justice the people who leave them behind.

CHAPTER 2

The Search for Hidden Prints

Every crime scene is a puzzle. Investigators work backward, using whatever clues remain at the scene, to figure out exactly what crime was committed, how it was done, and most importantly, who did it. The identity of the criminal is usually the last question to be answered, but it is the question the fingerprint expert is most interested in.

A fingerprint specialist is one of the investigators present at the scene of almost any major crime. Most crime scenes are peppered with fingerprints, and yet, this evidence is famously hard to find. It is also incredibly fragile. Simply brushing a soda can with a shirt sleeve could destroy a fingerprint, possibly the only print at the crime scene that would have been clear, complete, and usable. The practice of picking up a bottle or knife handle with a handkerchief, something investigators often do on TV, will almost surely destroy any prints that have been left behind. Real-life crime scene experts know how easy it is to destroy a print. They also realize that although they may gather many fingerprints at a crime scene, most are useless because they are too blurry, smudged, or overlapped with other prints to be clearly identified.

Skills for the Job

Fingerprint specialists must be patient, thorough, careful, and clever. Fingerprints may be numerous at a scene, but there is limited time to search for them. And not every print that is found will belong to the criminal. A murder scene in a family's living room, for example, will reveal countless prints, but most will belong to family members, friends, and other people who had a reason to be in the home recently. Because fingerprint

A door covered in fingerprint dust. Fingerprint experts often focus their search on the places where they are most likely to find prints, like doors and windows.

collectors have no way of knowing whose prints are found at a scene, they must identify the most likely places to find the *criminal's* prints. This takes skill and practice, and often, it forces the fingerprint specialist to think like a criminal, too.

In her book *Every Contact Leaves a Trace*, author Connie Fletcher quotes a latent print specialist who told her, "You have to keep an extremely open mind when you go into these places. Nothing's off limits. Think about what this person did, how they did it, where they were, what they would do."[9] Fingerprint specialists rarely have the time or resources to examine every surface at a scene, from furniture and windows to walls to the floor, so they focus on the things the criminal was most likely to have touched. Murder detectives, after examining the scene and figuring out what happened, often point the fingerprint collector to the most likely places to find prints. The place where the criminal entered the scene is usually the first stop. "You have to think like a crook," one fingerprint specialist told Fletcher. "How did he get in? The window's kind of high, so he probably grabbed up underneath and pulled himself up. You want to look for prints on the underside of the windowsill."[10]

Checking for Evidence

Fingerprint specialists learn to search a crime scene for objects that had to be touched. Specifically, they search for things that a criminal probably touched without gloves on. Objects that an untrained person might see as garbage are often treasures to a fingerprint expert. A candy wrapper or an opened envelope, for example, is a likely place to find a fingerprint. Tearing open objects like these requires the delicate touch of bare fingers. Even criminals who think far enough ahead to put gloves on will usually remove them to get at the contents of an item wrapped in paper.

Tools, handles, and other devices that are easier to use barehanded are also good places to begin searching for prints. Forensic specialist Allyn DiMeo says she once found a victim's fingerprint in a suspect's vehicle under the latch of the passenger door. She couldn't see underneath the latch, so she collected the all-important evidence entirely by feel, placing the tape and hoping to get a print. She was successful. "I found [the victim's] fingerprint, and the suspect said he didn't even know her," DiMeo says.[11] If DiMeo had not been in the habit of checking for prints on every surface a suspect or a victim might have touched, the case may have gone unsolved. Fingerprint experts like DiMeo learn to be clever out of necessity. Prints at crime scenes are easy to miss and most prints are altogether invisible, at least to the naked eye.

Prints in Hiding

Anything criminals touch with bare hands (or feet) could put them in jail. Friction skin can leave impressions on almost anything. Some of these prints are quite obvious, such as a print left in blood, paint, ink, or another substance. These are called patent prints, meaning they are readily visible. If all criminals were careless enough to leave at least one patent print at a crime scene, fingerprint experts would have a very easy job indeed. In fact, for murder investigators, a killer's print in the victim's blood is the most convenient form of evidence around.

Unfortunately, crime scene experts cannot rely on patent prints alone. A criminal with blood on his hands is probably going to notice it and attempt to wipe away the traces of his fingerprints before he leaves. Good, clean patent prints are therefore a lucky break for investigators. But clean hands, too, leave trails of telling prints. A criminal may grab something soft, such as wax, chewing gum, or a bar of soap, and leave a fingerprint behind. He may also be betrayed by his own sweat, because the thin layer of perspiration that helps friction skin to grip also stays behind on objects that are touched. These types of impressions are latent prints—those that are usually invisible to the naked eye. The word *latent* means to lie hidden or to escape notice, and this is exactly what latent fingerprints do unless a fingerprint expert knows how to find them.

Following a trail of sweat may not sound as exciting as looking for bloody handprints, but it is a fingerprint special-ist's main role at a crime scene. After all, when people are

A fingerprint expert dusts to make latent prints appear visible. Without the expert's skill the prints may go unexposed and a crime may go unsolved.

afraid of getting caught, they tend to sweat a great deal. This makes latent prints plentiful at the scene of many crimes. The fingerprint expert finds the best way to expose the hidden prints and to save them for later examination. The job requires cutting-edge chemistry and physics techniques that make it an interesting task.

The Right Light

Fingerprint matching and identification take place in a crime laboratory, not at a crime scene. Prints found at crimes scenes, therefore, must be preserved and taken to a lab for identification. Before this can be done, a specialist must find the latent prints. One of the simplest and most effective ways is by looking at surfaces from different angles. Crouching to look across a tabletop or kneeling to look straight across a freshly waxed floor will bring a surprising number of latent prints into focus. Windows, mirrors, and the surfaces of appliances are other place where prints can pop into view just by approaching from a different angle.

Magnifying glasses and flashlights, although basic, are standard tools for latent print specialists. Shining a flashlight at an angle nearly parallel to a surface will often reveal latent prints that are there, and the specialist can mark them to be collected later.

Sometimes, more powerful lights are needed. Specialists turn to high-intensity light sources such as quartz or xenon lamps that can bring tricky prints into view. Lights of different wavelengths and ultraviolet light are also used. The chemicals in human sweat fluoresce, or glow, under laser light, so some latent prints may stand out if a laser is pointed at them in a dark room. Sometimes, investigators find prints just by using alternative light sources and wearing special goggles. However, most fingerprints do not glow even under specialized light sources without the help of chemicals.

X-rays are another tool investigators may use to find latent prints at crime scenes. Three chemicals found in human sweat—chlorine, potassium, and sodium—react to the radiation. When

a beam of X-rays is aimed at an object or surface, the chemicals absorb the radiation. A special instrument then "reads" the data to create a digital image of the fingerprint.

Detection methods such as light sources and X-rays often tell latent print specialists where fingerprints are hiding at a scene. When the light is removed, the prints disappear again, but by then their locations have been marked for the next step in the process of print collection: making the existing prints permanent and useful.

Magnifying glasses and flashlights are standard tools used by fingerprint experts to uncover latent prints.

Prints and Powder

Finding the latent prints that have been left at a crime scene is only half the job. Knowing that a fingerprint exists on a surface does nothing to identify who left it there. The fingerprint specialist must bring the print's telltale papillary ridges into clear focus so the pattern can be analyzed and compared to other prints in a database. This process is called developing the print, and scientists are constantly finding new ways to do this on more surfaces than ever before.

There are two main ways to develop a latent print: by chemicals or by physical means. Physical methods include the brush and black powder that most people picture when they think of fingerprint science. The black powder is a fine carbon powder called lampblack, and it sticks to traces of perspiration and oil in the fingerprint to outline the ridges. Experts use brushes made of camel hair with bristles that are two to three inches long. These special brushes are incredibly soft, because fingerprints themselves are very delicate. A light touch is needed so it does not smudge and ruin a fingerprint during dusting.

Powders and camel-hair brushes are tools found in any latent print specialist's field kit, but they are far from the only things the print specialist will need. Developing prints with a brush and black powder works well on smooth, light-colored, sealed surfaces such as painted wood because the powder contrasts with the surface and brings out the fine details of the print. However, black powder does not work as well on dark objects. Instead, latent print specialists exchange the carbon powder for white or gray powders that show up against dark items. Fingerprints on objects with a colored, mottled, or patterned surface can be made visible with a fluorescent powder that reacts under a specialized light source.

Magnetic Device

Latent print experts can also exchange the standard camel-hair brush for a Magna Brush. This device has no bristles. Instead it uses a magnet to collect magnetic dusting powder. The powder itself forms the "bristles" of the Magna Brush, and the latent print expert then dusts these bristles of magnetic powder over a latent print. Unlike a camel-hair brush, the magnetic brush can work on porous surfaces—those that would soak up a drop

of water, such as leather and unfinished wood. Porous surfaces become clogged with standard fingerprint powder, which ruins the print. But magnetic brushes can be used on these surfaces, as well as on ceilings, walls, the undersides of tables, and other places that are hard to dust.

However, not even a Magna Brush can develop a fingerprint on every type of surface. And any powder method risks overdeveloping the print if the powder clumps up and makes the ridges difficult or impossible to see. Brush techniques can leave behind or ruin more than half of the fingerprints at a crime scene.

The fingerprints on this glove were revealed with the use of magnetic dusting powder. This type of powder is used on surfaces that are porous and may become clogged with the traditional fingerprint powder.

Dusting and Lifting a Fingerprint

Fingerprint technicians must make a permanent record of the prints they find at a crime scene. Developing a print with powder and lifting it with tape is one method. Here are the steps involved:

1 Dip the bristles of the brush into the powder. Do not touch the bristles with your fingers.

2 Fluff the brush bristles by rolling the handle between your palms.

3 In one stroke, gently move the brush across the fingerprint.

4 After the first stroke, determine the direction the print is going. Always brush in this direction to avoid streaking the print.

5 Blow away any extra powder.

6 Starting at the top of the print and moving slowly, apply a strip of tape. Make sure there are no wrinkles or bubbles.

7 When the tape is in place, press straight down on the entire surface of the print. Do not rub the tape.

8 Again starting at the top of the strip of tape and with a steady hand, carefully peel the tape off the print. Do not pause, as this could wrinkle the tape.

9 Smoothly lay the tape on the collection card and press down all the corners.

10 Number the card and jot down notes about where in the crime scene it was lifted.

11 Repeat the process if a second lift might get better results than the first.

Still, the brush-and-powder method is usually the easiest and cheapest way to develop prints, and at the scenes of less serious crimes (such as petty burglary), it may be all that investigators have the time and money to do. However, for serious crimes such as rapes and murders,, latent print specialists turn to chemistry.

A Chemical Touch

Chemicals solve some of the problems of the brush methods for developing prints. They can make the ridge patterns of fingerprints visible on a wider variety of objects and surfaces. However, the techniques can be complicated, and some of the equipment is not easily carried around. Some objects need to be taken back to a laboratory to be chemically processed for fingerprints—a bit of an inconvenience when the object is a dining room table or a kitchen oven. Latent print specialists have even been known to remove entire walls to be taken to a lab for chemical fingerprint processing.

Unlike powders, which stick to the ridges of a fingerprint, chemicals react with the print itself, often changing its color so that the ridge details can be easily seen. One of the oldest methods is iodine fuming. With this technique, the object bearing the fingerprint is placed in a cabinet with iodine crystals. The cabinet is heated, and the iodine crystals turn into a vapor that reacts with the print to make the ridge patterns visible.

Latent-print specialists also use a chemical called ninhydrin, which reacts with amino acids, an ingredient found in human sweat. Latent prints turn purple when ninhydrin is applied to them. Scientists made this discovery when trying to analyze fingerprints on paper—one of the most difficult surfaces on which to develop a fingerprint. Ninhydrin is easy to carry to a crime scene (it comes in aerosol cans), and it works even on very old fingerprints. In his book *Fingerprint Techniques*, Moenssens

A forensic scientist examines the fingerprints revealed on a gun after it underwent the iodine fuming process.

describes finding his own fingerprints with ninhydrin in a college textbook he had not touched in nine years.

Ninhydrin has one serious disadvantage: its fumes can cause splitting headaches. Understandably, latent-print specialists prefer to use other chemicals and avoid ninhydrin if they can. Silver nitrate works on many of the same surfaces as ninhydrin, including paper. The silver reacts with traces of salt in a fingerprint to form silver chloride. This glows under ultraviolet light to reveal the print's ridge patterns. However, silver nitrate and ninhydrin techniques often destroy the paper on which the fingerprint is found. A disadvantage of silver nitrate, in fact, is that it permanently marks almost anything it touches—even a fingerprint specialist's skin. If the paper itself is important evidence, latent print specialists must use other chemical procedures to get the print, or they must wait to process the print until the document has been copied or otherwise preserved.

Superglue Strength

Another chemical used to develop prints is the vapor of cyanoacrylate—otherwise known as superglue. Fuming with superglue has become a common technique for preserving fingerprints. An object is placed in an airtight tank with the superglue, which is heated to its boiling point so that it turns into

This handgun underwent the cyanoacrylate, or superglue, fuming process which produced the white markings seen and possibly fingerprints.

a vapor. As the superglue vapors condense, they turn back into superglue and stick to the fingerprint. The glue builds up on the print's ridges, hardening them. Sometimes, investigators will fume the entire inside of an automobile in this way. Specialists also use hand-held wands that heat a small cartridge with a mixture of superglue and fluorescent dye. The wand can be waved over a porous surface at a crime scene that would be difficult to dust with powder.

These inventions are important because they allow latent print experts to develop more prints directly at the scene of a crime. This is often preferable to taking an object back to the lab, because the fingerprint could be damaged during the move.

One distinct advantage of superglue fuming is that it makes a fragile print more durable. The superglue technique can be followed with traditional powder methods to make fingerprints even clearer and more visible because lightly brushing the treated print will no longer destroy it.

Metal Detection

Scientists are always finding new ways to develop stubborn or fragile fingerprints, and one of the newest techniques involves coating an object with a thin layer of gold and zinc to bring a hidden fingerprint into focus. This is called vacuum metal deposition (VMD) because it is done inside a vacuum chamber. It enables specialists to recover prints from surfaces that were once very difficult or even impossible to fingerprint. Using VMD, fingerprint experts can develop high-quality prints on substances such as leather, photographs and their negatives, glass, and smooth fabrics like nylon. The VMD technique develops more prints, and prints of better quality, than most other methods, including superglue and fluorescent dyes.

Although the technology is expensive and not yet available to all police departments, forensic specialist Allyn DiMeo describes VMD as one of the most significant breakthroughs in fingerprint science to date. "You can use it when all else fails," she says, "even on clothing like a windbreaker or satin underwear."[12]

The concept of fingerprints may not be new to crime science, but fingerprint specialists continue to study and invent new techniques that keep fingerprints at the front of the crime science field. There are many types of surfaces that scientists are still scrambling to fingerprint well, because any undeveloped fingerprint could allow a criminal to go free.

Fragile Paper

Latent print specialists never know what surfaces they will be asked to process for prints, but some objects are more frustrating than others. The one item at a crime scene on which prints are most likely to be found may also be the most difficult item to process.

Even with the help of silver nitrate and ninhydrin, paper remains one of the touchiest materials for an investigator to process. This is unfortunate, because criminals touch a great deal of paper, whether they are forging documents, writing checks, opening envelopes, or drafting ransom notes—any of which can make the paper itself valuable evidence as well.

Developing prints on paper without ruining the document is now possible with a chemical called DFO (short for 1,8-diazafluoreneone). DFO can develop a print in just thirty minutes without the purple stains (and the headaches) ninhydrin leaves behind. Seeing the DFO-treated print requires a specialized light source, but the advantages are clear. "A document can be examined but show no visible evidence that it was examined," says Graham Ford, a certified latent print examiner who has worked for Scotland Yard and the Oklahoma State Bureau of Investigation.[13] Not only does the paper remain readable when DFO is used, undercover investigators can use the technique on items that belong to the suspect, and he or she will be none the wiser.

DFO also exposes more than twice the number of prints that can be seen with ninhydrin. Ford calls DFO "the best new technique to hit the fingerprint development lab arena."[14]

Challenging Surfaces

A fingerprint expert adjusts a piece of paper containing latent fingerprints under a light. It is now possible for forensic scientists to find latent fingerprints on paper with the use of a chemical called DFO and a special light.

Other surfaces that challenge fingerprint specialists include plastic bags (which are common in drug-related crimes), currency such as coins and bills, and latex (although specialists are now able to recover fingerprints from inside a latex glove). A chemical called Sudan Black can help experts develop prints on oily surfaces. Other chemicals are used to dye and enhance prints that have been left in blood. And a substance called sticky-slide powder, when combined with a mixture of soap and black or gray powder, can even develop prints left on adhesive surfaces such as the sticky side of a piece of duct tape that a kidnapper used to bind his victim.

Human skin is probably the most difficult surface to fingerprint, and it is the one that scientists are studying most anxiously. After all, a murder victim's body will almost certainly bear impressions of the killer—a palm print, a fingerprint, a footprint. The ability to find these prints will be the ticket to solving many a grisly case. But it has never been possible to fingerprint human skin successfully. The chemicals used to develop fingerprints react with natural oils and substances in human skin and sweat, so they also react with the victim's skin instead of just the remaining fingerprint.

However, this is changing. Crime scientists are on the brink of discovering fail-proof ways to get a criminal's prints from the

Although a murder victim's body, like this hand, will probably contain impressions from the killer, it is not yet possible to obtain fingerprints from the human skin.

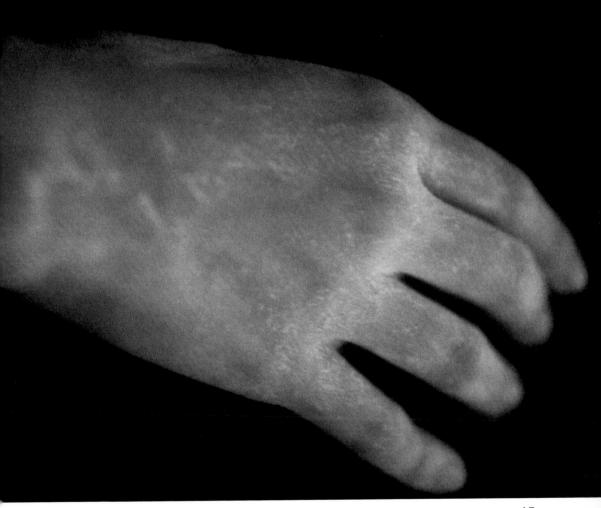

skin of a victim. But they face many challenges. "Skin isn't the best surface under any circumstances," says Genge.

"It stretches, which means that prints can be so distorted it's impossible to make any match. If the victim doesn't die, skin might shed the layer where investigators are hoping to find the print. It's not all that unusual for areas of contact between suspects and victims to include injuries, and injuries are usually treated by a variety of people (who often leave prints of their own). All of these things destroy prints."[15]

Fingers as Clues

Criminals have been known to leave their fingerprints behind—literally. In their book *Crime Science: Methods of Forensic Detection*, authors Joe Nickell and John F. Fischer relate the following ghastly examples:

A burglar in Cochise County, Arizona, left his crowbar—and the skin from his finger—alongside the safe he had robbed. He was later identified by ridges on the skin scrap and sent to Arizona State Penitentiary.

A would-be thief left an entire finger dangling from the iron spike of a gate that protected a London warehouse. The ill-fated appendage was discovered by a constable from Scotland Yard, who immediately took it to the Fingerprint Bureau. The resulting fingerprint was soon matched to that of a well-known burglar—who happened to be missing his right ring finger.

An attempted robbery of a bank in Pittsburgh, Pennsylvania, ended tragically for the burglar when he detonated the bomb he was carrying. Among the bits of him that remained, police found a right hand. The disembodied fingers were inked and printed, and they matched those of a seasoned criminal.

In spite of the challenges, fingerprint specialists are not giving up. In recent years, human corpses have been fumed with superglue and even dusted for fingerprints using basic lampblack powder—and some of these experiments have produced prints that were collected successfully. It may not be long before murder victims themselves can reveal the friction-skin traces of their killers.

Print Preservation

Making prints permanent is perhaps the most important step in developing them. Because eventually the prints will be scanned into a computer, handled and examined by identification

A crime scene investigator lifts fingerprints. The process of lifting is used to make fingerprints as permanent and durable as possible so they can be used in court as evidence.

experts at the lab, and possibly even carried into a courtroom as evidence, it is important to make them as permanent and durable as possible. This traditionally has been done by a process called lifting.

A print that has been developed with powder is taken from the crime scene by physically peeling up the print and the powder or other substance that is sticking to it. This is done with the help of adhesive tape, which is applied over the print, peeled away, and then attached to a card. The print is now preserved and can be handled safely during identification.

Because powders are used only on certain types of surfaces, the tape-lifting method is not useful for fingerprints developed on porous surfaces (or with chemicals or other methods). For these types of prints, photography is often the best method for making a permanent and usable record of the evidence. Fingerprint photography uses special cameras and film that can capture images of the prints at various angles, as well as ridge details that have been enhanced with chemicals that glow or fluoresce. An added benefit of photographs is that they record the location and position of the fingerprint on the actual object. This can be useful if investigators later have questions about where or how a suspect's fingerprint might have been left behind.

A Messy Process

Small as latent prints are, finding and developing prints at a crime scene creates a big mess. Fingerprinting techniques can do thousands of dollars of damage to a home or business. By spreading around chemicals, dyes, powders, or thin films of metal, latent print experts leave a crime scene in far worse condition than when they found it. Furniture, floors, walls, and other surfaces are often destroyed in an expert's search for invisible prints. "Latent print work, especially with nonporous items or surfaces in a house, is the last thing we do at a scene," one latent print specialist told Fletcher. "Once we start throwing powder around, we're basically going to destroy that place.

Becoming a Forensic Photographer

Job Description:
A forensic photographer documents crime scenes and takes part in criminal investigations using various types of cameras and video equipment. Using specialized light sources, ultraviolet films, x-rays, microscopes, and other technology, the forensic photographer creates a legal record of evidence at the scene of a crime and in the crime laboratory.

Education:
A degree from a four-year college with major coursework in photography, or digital imaging and forensic science is preferred. Because this is a highly technical field, strong working knowledge of cameras, lighting, video and digital equipment, and the use of cameras to capture fluorescent and other types of images is essential.

Qualifications:
Forensic photographers must have excellent interpersonal skills for photographing people and must be able to learn new technology quickly. They should be well organized and mechanically inclined, have great hand-eye coordination, and be willing to spend a lot of time learning new techniques of the trade.

Additional Information:
Half of all forensic photographers are self-employed and work as independent freelancers. Forensic photographers have extremely varied working hours and environments and must be willing to work anywhere and at any hour of the day or night.

Salary:
$15,000 per year for part-time, freelance photographers to $50,000 per year for full-time photographers

We're going to be tracking powder everywhere and it gets to be a real mess."[16]

Still, wherever they are collected, and by whatever means, the fingerprints processed at a crime scene are central to the investigation of the crime. Armed with evidence in the form of tiny skin swirls, the latent print expert will head back to the lab. There, the next step of fingerprint processing begins … tracking down the person whose prints match the evidence.

CHAPTER 3

Making an Identification

Latent print specialists are usually lugging a lot of fingerprints when they return from a crime scene. Some of these will have been lifted (peeled from a surface) using adhesive tape that is then pressed onto a card. Others will have been photographed, and a few may still be attached to the items on which they were discovered—a car, a table, a chunk of plaster from a wall. At this point, the crime scene technicians have done their job. The rest of the fingerprint work is performed in the crime lab by fingerprint examiners—the experts in fingerprint classification.

No two fingerprints are exactly the same, and this fact is at the core of a fingerprint examiner's efforts. Each and every print collected at a crime scene must be compared to other fingerprints in the hope of finding a match that will prove a suspect was at the scene. Whether fingerprint evidence will help to solve a crime depends on the particular case. "If a second print is already available," says Genge, "a direct visual inspection of the two prints begins. If not—the print will have to go into the database in search of a match elsewhere."[17]

Not all fingerprints collected at a crime scene will match those of the police's prime suspect. It may be that all the latent prints belong to people who had an honest reason to be at the scene recently. The fingerprint examiner may also find it impossible to work with some prints. After all, criminals do not leave their prints behind on purpose. They are not trying to deposit perfect impressions that will help examiners solve the crime. Prints from a crime scene are often smudged or overlapping other prints, or not enough of the fingerprint is left behind to be useful for making a comparison.

40 MILLION:

Number of fingerprint comparisons made in the United States each year

There is a world of difference between a fingerprint taken carefully and methodically at a police station and a latent fingerprint left by accident on a surface at the scene of a crime, says Cole. He explains, "The detective must match this distorted crime scene print to an inked print, taken under pristine 'laboratory' conditions, to the exclusion of all other fingerprints in the world."[18] Prints of poor quality are a constant nuisance for fingerprint examiners. However, the most frustrating part of their work may be when a lone print, perfect and clear, *is* left behind at a scene—but it matches no fingerprint on file. The fingerprint lab must then wait and hope for a future match to be entered into its database. A matching print and the criminal who belongs to it may never turn up. Sometimes, though, fingerprint examiners are able to quickly match a print from a crime scene to the print of a person the police already suspect. Or perhaps the print belongs to none of the suspects in the crime, but it matches a print in a database, thus pointing police toward a person they otherwise did not suspect.

Finding a Lead

Between 1984 and 1985, the citizens of Los Angeles were afraid to go to sleep. A serial killer was on the loose, shooting men and raping women in their homes in the middle of the night and leaving satanic symbols in his wake. Finally, after long months of searching for a clue about the man's identity, police got a break when a victim was able to write down the license plate number of the killer's escape vehicle. The car had been stolen, and police found it abandoned in a parking lot. One suspicious fingerprint was recovered from the car, and a database search matched it to Richard Ramirez, whose only previous arrest had been for a minor traffic violation. Ramirez was arrested, and more evidence

It was a recovered fingerprint that allowed police to arrest and eventually convict Richard Ramirez of killing sixteen people in 1984 and 1985 in Los Angeles, California.

BK 7867407 12-12-84

LOS ANGELES POLICE = JAIL - F

was found linking him to the murders. That single fingerprint led to one of the longest trials in U.S. history, and Ramirez was given the death penalty in 1989 for killing sixteen people and assaulting twenty-four others.

Latent prints can be invaluable leads in an unsolved case like Ramirez's. These are the scenarios that scare criminals and keep fingerprint examiners going day after day at a job that requires long hours of staring at friction ridges, looking for telling similarities.

Common Patterns

Using a fingerprint to confirm someone's identity—for example, to prove that a corpse discovered in a river is that of a woman who went missing two weeks ago—is fairly easy. Investigators get prints for the missing person from a personal object or from the person's home. The two sets of prints are compared, and an expert determines whether they match or not.

But what if the corpse's fingerprints do not match those of the missing woman? They must then be used to discover the identity of an unknown person. This is a lot more difficult. Police have to compare the corpse's prints to all of the fingerprints they have on file. This could mean making thousands or even millions of comparisons.

In the early 1900s, when the science of fingerprinting was still new, police officers did these kinds of comparisons by hand, sifting through hundreds or thousands of fingerprints, one at a time, looking for a match. It was a miserably dreary job, but after spending so much time staring at prints, examiners realized that the prints fell into general categories based on the shapes their ridges formed. It was easy to tell if a print had a peak in the middle of its pattern, for example, and if it did, there was no need to compare it to all of the prints that did not have a peak.

Sir Edward Richard Henry, Scotland Yard's fingerprinting pioneer, used these basic similarities to create a detailed classification system for fingerprints in the early 1900s. It is still the system used by experts today. The Henry system of classification is based on math, and although Henry did not have computers in mind in the early 1900s, his system works perfectly with today's computerized databases. By scanning the fingerprint and coding it based on its major features, detectives quickly narrow down the number of prints computers have to compare.

The Henry classification system divides fingerprints into three basic patterns: arches, loops, and whorls. In an arch pattern, the ridge lines rise in the middle in what looks like a hill. This hill can be either plain (a smooth rise) or tented (rising sharply upward to form a peak). About 5 to 10 percent of all fingerprint patterns are tents.

In a loop pattern, the ridge lines in the print turn back on themselves to form a loop. Loops are further classified by whether they flow toward the pinky finger (ulnar loops, named after the ulna bone of the forearm) or toward the thumb (radial loops, named after the radius bone of the forearm). Loops are the most common fingerprint pattern. Roughly two-thirds of all prints are loops.

In the third pattern type—a whorl—the ridges form a circle or a spiral around a central point in the fingerprint. Whorls can take the shape of ovals or any other variation of a circle. They make up about one-third of all fingerprint patterns.

Henry's classification system further divides the three main categories of prints—arches, loops, and whorls—into 1,024 total groups based on more specific details. When a person's fingerprints are taken, each print is given a number that depends on its pattern and which of the ten fingers it is. These numbers break fingerprints into different classes. When it is necessary to make a fingerprint comparison, the search will involve only those prints in a database that have the same number value based on their main features. Thus, the search for a match always moves from general characteristics to more specific similarities.

Automated Searches

Henry's classification system has been one of the greatest advances in crime science. Originally designed to make life easier for police officers who had the unpopular job of sorting

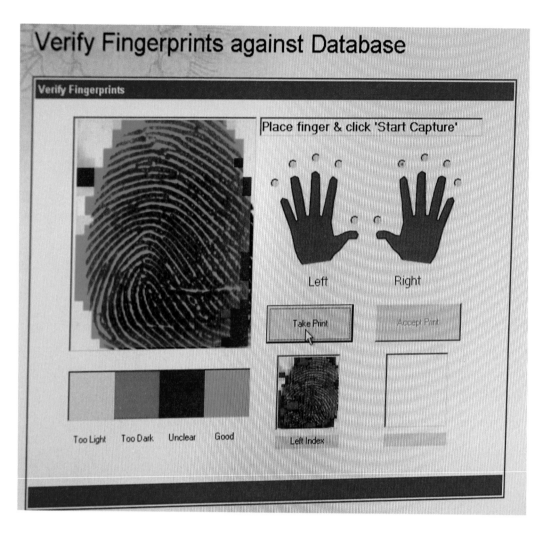

A record from the automated fingerprint identification system, or AFIS. This system uses computers to search large numbers of fingerprint files in a matter of seconds.

through fingerprint cards one at a time, the system today allows computers to search ever-growing files of fingerprints in a matter of seconds. And speed is of the essence when trying to solve a crime. "In order to be useful, fingerprints must be filed in great quantity, and searching for a match must be accomplished as quickly as possible," say Nickell and Fischer in *Crime Science: Methods of Forensic Detection.*[19] This was the reasoning behind the development of the automated fingerprint identification system, or AFIS. A computer scans fingerprints into digital images and stores the ridge details as a geometric pattern. With this information, the system can read an unknown fingerprint (such as one from a crime scene) and quickly search fingerprint files to bring up a handful of prints that are the closest geometric matches.

The fingerprints collected at a crime scene are always compared first to the prints of the victim, the top suspects in the case, and anyone else who had a reason to be at the scene recently, such as paramedics, police officers, and people who live or work at the crime scene. Fingerprints that match none of these people are then entered into an automated identification system, and a computer compares them to all the ten-print cards that have ever been taken during arrests and background checks. Prints similar to a crime scene print, called candidates, are pulled up, and a fingerprint examiner looks closely at them to see if one matches the unknown print.

When a matching fingerprint is found, it is called a hit. If no hit is made, the database stores the unidentified print and compares it to unmatched prints from other crimes. By constantly comparing database records this way, AFIS can link

Spanning a Nation with Fingerprints

J. Edgar Hoover, former director of the FBI, planned and instituted a national system of identification based on a core set of about one million prints in the first half of the twentieth century. The country was becoming more mobile, as cars, highways, and even airplanes made it easy for criminals to commit crimes in one place, leave their fingerprints behind, and quickly move on with little fear of being captured by their prints. Hoover wanted a national fingerprint system that made criminals' fingerprint records easy for any police officer in the country to access. He got his wish when the fingerprint database went national, and crimes that local police forces had been working on for years were suddenly able to be solved in days.

A police officer demonstrates the use of an IBIS, a portable fingerprinting device that allows officers to scan and search fingerprints wirelessly in the field.

crimes that police might never have connected. AFIS can also help solve crimes that took place many years ago.

Automated fingerprint searches have been used since the 1970s, but they are getting faster and more reliable all the time. Today's computers can compare a crime-scene fingerprint to half a million other prints in less than a second. In the city of Los Angeles, where police have nearly two million fingerprint cards on file, a computer can find a few likely matches in about twenty minutes. In the days before computers, a fingerprint technician would have spent almost seventy years to finish the same task.

AFIS is gaining ground in the race against criminals. "In the future, I foresee these [AFIS] devices being portable, able to be taken to the crime scene, and IDs made on the spot," says Jones.[20] In fact, police officers in Ontario, California, have been using an early form of such a system since 2003, when they started carrying hand-held information-based identification systems (IBIS). With these devices, a police officer can scan fingerprints and search a fingerprint database within minutes to confirm whether a suspect is as innocent as he claims to be.

Computers Catching Criminals

Computers are also used to clear up fingerprints themselves. High-resolution monitors and digital photography programs can help to enhance faint, smudged, or blurry fingerprints. With this technology, examiners are able to clarify and use more prints from crime scenes, even when the quality of the prints is poor.

Computers also accompany fingerprint examiners in court. When testifying that a defendant's prints match (or do not match) the prints found at a crime scene, examiners often use computer technology to present their evidence to the jury. Lawyers on TV often make their fingerprint cases by laying a see-through image of one fingerprint pattern over another. In his article "How Fingerprint Scanners Work," Harris explains that in real life, this is rarely possible. "Smudging can make two images of the same print look pretty different," Harris says. "So you're rarely going to get a perfect image overlay."[21] With the help of computers, however, two fingerprint images can be easily enlarged and placed side by side on a viewing screen using digital photography. This process is much more jury-friendly than overhead projectors or paper photocopies.

At the crime scene, at the lab, and in the courtroom, computers have become one of a fingerprint examiner's best weapons for matching prints and nailing criminals. Computers cannot, however, replace fingerprint examiners themselves. Fingerprints and the criminals who made them are human, and ultimately, it takes a human to link the two. Computers have radically changed the field of fingerprint science, but it is always a fingerprint expert who makes the match.

Expert Opinion

Declaring that two fingerprints came from the same finger is a big responsibility. A person's very life could hang on a fingerprint examiner's opinion. Fingerprint evidence has led many a jury to a verdict of guilty.

It is true that no two fingerprints are exactly alike, but this does not mean that telling them apart is easy. Most whorls, arches, and loops look very much like other whorls, arches, and loops. The significant differences are found in the minutiae—tiny details such as where friction ridges start and end, where they meet, and where they branch—and how close these details are to one another in a given print.

To work out whether two fingerprints came from the same finger, experts look at several things. First, both prints must fall into the same category based on whether they arch, loop, or whorl and the way these patterns take shape. Second, both prints must be complete enough to make a comparison. Finally, the fingerprint examiner looks closely at the minutiae of both prints. The defining details in the friction ridges must be the same relative direction and distance from each other for the prints to be declared a match. "The basic idea is to measure the relative positions of minutiae, in the same sort of way you might recognize a part of the sky by the relative positions of the stars," says Harris.[22]

Fingerprint examiners often imagine or draw straight lines through the images they are comparing. This helps them make sure that the minutiae of both prints—the places where the friction ridges join, split, and change direction—are not only in line with each other but are the same distance from one another in both samples.

By the Numbers

7,000:

Number of new records the FBI adds to its fingerprint files every day

---

Fortunately for examiners, an entire fingerprint is not always necessary to make a match. As experts look at the minutiae of two fingerprints, they keep a tally of the details that are identical and the same distance (or number of ridges apart) in the two prints. When a certain number of similarities have been counted, the prints are considered to match. According to the FBI, any two fingerprints having as many as fourteen identical ridge characteristics will contain no dissimilarities; the prints must have come from the same finger. Even if one of the prints is not complete, and even if the prints have been distorted by smearing, smudging, overlapping with other prints, or any other form of interference, two prints with this many similarities can still be declared a match.

An FBI fingerprint examiner teaches a class on fingerprinting. Fingerprint experts train for years before they are able to testify in court on their findings in the field.

When fingerprint examiners do decide that two prints are from the same source, it is with complete certainty. If even one difference exists between two prints, it means they simply do not match. "Examiners don't think in any percentages except zero and one hundred," says Genge.[23] Two prints are either a perfect match or a mismatch—there is no in-between.

Fingerprint examiners stake their reputation on their opinion, and it is a reputation they must earn. They train for years to be called fingerprint experts and to gain the status they need to appear as witnesses in court. Interpreting and comparing latent fingerprints requires a mix of instinct and extensive training. Anyone can look at two fingerprints and see some similarities and differences, but only an expert can compare latent and inked fingerprints and see the details that inexperienced observers miss. "A fingerprint expert can tell apart the marks of two digits more easily than he can differentiate two people's faces," says Beavan. "The facial features of two identical twins … can be mistaken, but their fingerprints can never be confused by a trained expert."[24]

Fingerprints in Court

"Probably the best-known activity of the FBI, dramatized in thousands of gangster films and television dramas for two thirds of a century, is related to fingerprints," say Douglas Ubelaker and Henry Scammell in their book *Bones: A Forensic Detective's Casebook*. "The Identification Division … has maintained world leadership in the size and utility of its collection ever since."[25] There is enormous demand for fingerprint analysis in the United States. Forty million comparisons are made every year, and computers are increasingly being used to help examiners handle this enormous workload.

Fingerprints, and the experts who testify about them, are a long-standing topic of debate in the courtroom. Since the earliest days of fingerprint evidence, defense lawyers have been trying to invalidate the technique. A century ago, they argued that investigators had not looked at enough fingerprints to

Becoming a Latent Print Examiner:

Job Description:
Latent print examiners are experts who compare complete and partial latent prints (that have been lifted from or developed on objects at crime scenes) with possible matching prints from a database. They often testify in court as expert witnesses.

Education:
Latent print examiners typically have at least a high school diploma. Most have completed college-level programs in biology, chemistry, criminal justice, or forensic science. Their course work must include the Henry System of fingerprint classification.

Qualifications:
To become a latent print examiner, a candidate must receive formal training in the standard techniques for classifying and filing inked fingerprints. At least three years of full-time experience finding, developing, lifting, and preserving latent prints at crime scenes is required. To become a certified latent print examiner (CLPE), a candidate must take and pass the rigorous six-hour exam given by the International Association of Identification.

Additional Information:
Because they are often called on to be expert witnesses in court, latent print examiners need strong deductive reasoning and public speaking skills.

Salary:
$50,000 to $160,000 per year.

determine that no two prints could ever be identical matches. These days, others argue that *too many* fingerprints have been collected for examiners to make identical matches. With forty million comparisons made each year, they say, the odds are considerable that examiners and the computers they use might slip up from time to time and make a false comparison.

Mistakes can be made when using a computer program to enhance a poor-quality print or when scanning fingerprints and entering them into a database. The computer could accidentally file a print in the wrong category, and thus overlook it altogether when searching for a match. There could be problems anywhere in the computerized process of indexing, storing, or retrieving fingerprints, and fingerprint examiners may be accused in court of relying too heavily on computers for evidence.

A fingerprint expert from the ATF testifies for the prosecution in the case against Washington D.C.-area sniper suspect John Allen Muhammad.

In addition, fingerprint examiners themselves have always been judged on their ability to declare a match between two prints. A computer may narrow down the millions of possible prints to a few that might match, but "it's humans who sit in the lab and stare at each print, identifying landmarks in the mass of swirls and ultimately declaring a match or mismatch," says Genge.[26] Since the early days of fingerprint evidence, examiners have come under fire in the courtroom—just how reliable *is* their opinion?

It seems that some fingerprint experts make decisions more consistently than others. One study showed that several experts changed their minds about whether two fingerprints were a match. They initially identified the prints as from the same source, but later, when examining the same two prints again, they decided the prints did not match at all.

A Second Opinion

For this and other reasons, fingerprint examiners almost always seek a second opinion. At most agencies, a match is not declared a match until it is verified by another expert. Backed by the opinions of two qualified examiners, fingerprint evidence is generally strong enough to withstand arguments in the courtroom.

Fingerprint evidence is strengthened by the fact that not anyone can be considered an expert. A fingerprint examiner usually trains for years with an experienced latent print specialist before he or she works unsupervised to examine prints from crime scenes. To get certified by the International Association of Identification, latent print examiners then must take a six-hour exam. Fewer than half of all people who take this test pass it and become certified.

When a certified fingerprint examiner takes the stand, the evidence he or she presents is backed by years of extremely hard training and study. Ultimately, though, juries look at the evidence presented and make their own decisions. Usually, these decisions follow the advice of the fingerprint experts.

From crime scene to courtroom, the process of finding, developing, collecting, and comparing fingerprints remains one of the most important jobs in criminal identification. Fingerprint experts hold a position of high esteem in the criminology field.

CHAPTER 4

Impressions

Fingerprints top the list of vital evidence that crime scene experts hope to collect: they can be linked to one and only one person, and they can be used to track down a criminal's identity. The same usually cannot be said for shoe prints, tire tracks, and other impression evidence. Any number of people could wear a certain style of shoe, for example. Although the FBI keeps a large database of tire tracks, proving that one and only one vehicle could possibly have left the tracks found at a crime scene may turn out to be an impossible task.

Just the same, there are countless ways for a criminal to make an impression, and many a crook has been caught by prints that did not come from his fingertips. Impression evidence can sometimes tell crime scene experts things that even fingerprints cannot. The scene of any major crime, therefore, is also combed for impressions made by objects other than fingers.

Footprints

Many criminals are tripped up by their own feet. The soles and toes, after all, are also covered in friction skin. Very few inked footprints are ever stored in police databases, so it is not likely that a criminal's identity will be discovered by a footprint alone. However, if police have a suspect in mind, prints can be taken from that person's feet and compared to the print from the crime scene. Because all friction skin is completely unique, a footprint match would hold up in court as well as any fingerprint identification. If the footprints do not match, of course, the suspect's name would be cleared.

Most footprints at crime scenes, though, are made not by bare feet but by shoes. Even when investigators are able to determine the specific brand and size of the shoe, it is tricky to prove which *exact* shoe left the print in question, out of all shoes of that brand and size that have ever been made. "*Individualization* is the key word in forensic work," says Genge. "Everyone wants evidence that points to one-and only one-item, suspect, or victim."[27] Just the same, detectives armed with shoe prints have valuable information they can use. Perhaps the particular shoe is rare-something only a bicyclist would wear, for example. Or maybe the shoe's sole is worn down on one side, suggesting its wearer has a limp. Such details about a shoe help crime scene experts to narrow down their list of suspects based on the impressions they have collected.

What we're doing during the examination is comparing it with the suspects' shoes," says William Bodziak, a former FBI agent and footwear specialist who helped organize a large FBI database of shoe soles. "We will make test impressions of the suspects' shoes and compare the specific size and design features. It does not mean that the person's shoe caused the impression because thousands of other shoes could have done the same, but it is very important evidence."[28]

When former football star O. J. Simpson was on trial for murder in the 1990s, investigators lifted bloody shoe prints from the front walkway of the murder scene. They could tell from the shape of the sole that these were not athletic shoes, but expensive Italian shoes. Photographs of the bloody shoe prints were faxed to nearly eighty companies that made or imported such shoes. One owner responded, claiming that the shoe prints at the crime scene had definitely come from a pair that his company made and were definitely a size twelve—Simpson's size. The company owner also told investigators that exactly 299 pairs of those shoes in

By the Numbers

2 OUT OF 5:

Proportion of crime scenes at which investigators find shoe impression evidence

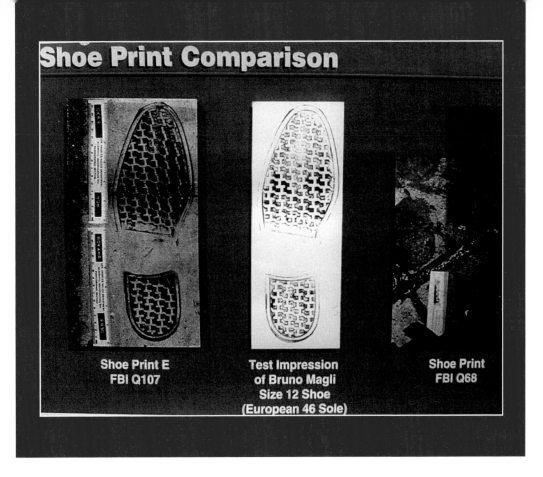

Shoe Print Comparison

Shoe Print E
FBI Q107

**Test Impression
of Bruno Magli
Size 12 Shoe
(European 46 Sole)**

**Shoe Print
FBI Q68**

that size had been sold in the United States, and that only forty stores carried them. One of these was Bloomingdale's, where Simpson was known to buy a lot of his shoes. From shoe prints alone, investigators were able to get a strong piece of evidence.

A photograph of the shoe print comparison evidence used in the trial of O.J. Simpson. The shoe prints ended up being a key piece of evidence in the trial.

A Useful Lead

Surprisingly, although shoe prints can often prove guilt in a crime, they are one area of evidence where most criminals never think to cover their tracks. "Criminals have become smarter and wiser by beginning to frequently wear protection over their hands to avoid leaving fingerprints," says certified latent print examiner Dwayne S. Hilderbrand in his book *Footwear: The Missed Evidence.* "However, they are rarely aware of, or make little attempt to conceal footwear."[29]

Footprints also speak volumes about how the crime was committed and how the criminal got away. Investigators with a sharp

Size And Scale

With any impression, crime scene experts have to think in terms of scale. All fingerprints are approximately the same size, but the dimensions of shoe prints, tire tracks, and other impressions can vary greatly. It is crucial for forensic experts to establish the size of an image while they are taking pictures of it for later use in the crime lab or in court. This is usually done by laying a ruler next to the object before photographing it, so that the picture will show exactly how long or wide the impression is. If a ruler is not available, investigators use any object that is a standard size, such as a credit card or a dollar bill.

eye for impressions can learn where someone entered the scene, which direction they went when they left, and whether they ran or walked. The distance between the footprints can also tell detectives the approximate height of the person who made them.

A lucky investigator might even be able to follow a trail of footprints to a second crime scene, to the location of a body, or to tire tracks made by a getaway car-which are other forms of evidence. Much like shoe prints, tire tracks can give away sizes, brands, and models. The distance between the tracks can narrow down the type of vehicle that made them. Even skid marks can be evidence, telling police how fast a car might have been going when it entewred or left the crime scene and whether it had four-wheel drive.

Criminal Clothing

When impression experts examine a crime scene, they also look for markings left by clothing other than shoes. Important evidence has taken the form of patterns left by corduroy pants where the criminal knelt on a dusty floor, for example. And in 1998, a man in New York State was caught by the impressions that the fabric tufts on his socks made at the scene of his stepmother's murder.

More common, however, are impressions made by gloves. Criminals who think they are outsmarting fingerprint specialists by covering their hands still leave plenty of evidence behind. Impression experts can learn important details, just from gloves themselves. Tears, snags, holes, and imperfections in the glove fabric can all make an impression unique. Gloves made out of leather often have specific creases or wrinkles based on the way they fit their owner's hands. If investigators can track down a suspect's gloves and match the details with the impressions left at the crime scene, those gloves can help prove guilt as surely as the fingerprints they were worn to conceal. "Such impressions are developed, photographed, and collected just as if they were fingerprints because they may be their equivalents," say Nickell and Fischer.[30]

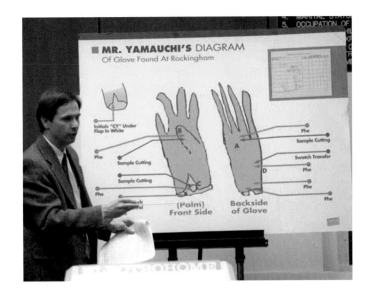

Although criminals may wear gloves to prevent leaving fingerprints, the gloves themselves may leave their own evidence behind that forensic scientists can use to reveal a suspect.

Body Impressions

Many criminals put a lot of effort into masking their fingerprints, but few give as much thought to masking other body parts, such as lips and ears. Crime scientists have been trying to determine whether ear or lip prints can reliably identify who made them. Ear prints are sometimes found on doors or walls that criminals have leaned against to hear what is going on in another room. Lip impressions are often left behind on things such as cigarettes and drink containers. So far, these kinds of impressions have not proved as useful as fingerprints, shoe prints, and glove prints in identifying crooks. Suspects have, however, been cleared of crimes when their ear prints

Freed By a Glove

During the O. J. Simpson murder trial, a glove impression was presented to the jury. It was clear to jurists that the specific glove they were looking at was the one that made the impression at the crime scene. They also believed that the glove could not have fit on Simpson's hand.

clearly did not match the ones left at the crime scene because of differences in shape or size.

Palm prints, too, are often overlooked by criminals concerned only with covering their fingers. Like the soles of the feet, the palms of the hands are covered with friction skin. Graham Ford describes a peculiar case in the 1980s in which palm prints were the chief evidence in the search for Michael Fagan, a crafty burglar who gained access to one of the most secure buildings in the world. "My most interesting case was the forced entry in the Queen's residence at Buckingham Palace," Ford says.

> Whilst burglary is not necessarily considered a 'major' crime, the fact that the intruder was able to get past all the security and subsequently made it into the Queen's bedroom, sat on the bed, and spoke with the Queen, it was treated most seriously.[31]

The intruder's palm prints were identified on the window sill where he entered the building after climbing a gutter downspout. "Palm prints are just as valuable for identification and evidence as are fingerprints and should never be overlooked as a source for the identification of a perpetrator," Ford says.

Bite Marks

Another type of bodily impression that can prove useful for identifying criminals is a bite mark. Teeth impressions are often left
behind at crime scenes, perhaps on a piece of chewed gum or on
an apple with a bite taken out of it. Dental impressions can be
made of a suspect's teeth for comparison. Unlike fingerprints,
matching bite marks do not necessarily mean that the suspect left
the tooth marks found at the crime scene. It is possible, if unlikely,
that two or more people can have nearly identical teeth and bite
marks. Just the same, many criminals have been captured because
their tooth impressions were linked to the crime.

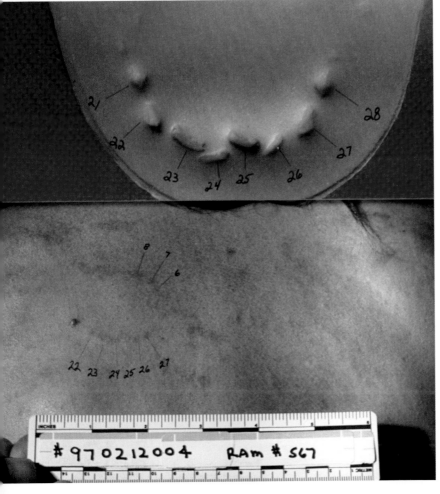

Like fingerprints, teeth marks may be used to identify suspects. The top photo shows impressions made by a suspect, which supposedly correspond to the numbered marks made on the victim's back, shown in the bottom photo.

Famed serial killer Ted Bundy, who is thought to have murdered forty to fifty women in the 1970s, is one example. Bundy was a brilliant criminal who never left a single fingerprint at any of his crime scenes. But when he bit one of his victims during an attack, he left behind his tooth impressions. These were measured and photographed, and when Bundy finally went to trial, the jury was able to compare casts and photographs of his teeth with pictures of the bite marks. This evidence was enough to convict Bundy, who was put to death in the electric chair in 1989.

Impressions Come First

Finding and collecting impressions is usually one of the very first things done at a crime scene. Impressions are often very fragile, especially those found outdoors. A change in weather-rain, wind, or melting snow—can permanently erase this evidence. As multiple investigators enter a crime scene to look for evidence of various kinds, they can also disrupt or destroy some of the impression evidence that is left there.

For these reasons, the first investigator to arrive at a crime scene usually inspects the area for impressions, marking them for later documentation and collection. Crime scene experts often take a careful path through a crime scene, being careful to retrace their own steps by walking exactly in their own footprints so that they disturb as little of the ground or floor as possible.

Finding impressions at a crime scene is much like finding fingerprints. Experts use many of the same techniques. They look first for so-called "plastic" prints, those that have been pressed into a surface so that they are essentially three-dimensional. Footprints left in mud or snow are good examples, but plastic prints can also be left in surfaces such as warm asphalt.

Some impressions are more difficult to see, but shining a flashlight across a floor or other surface can make many of them visible. Experts sometimes use finger-print powders to make impressions stand out so they are easier to preserve or photograph. Treating impressions in this way can make them more useful in attempts to solve a crime or convince a jury.

Casting Prints

Some impressions are left in mud, wet sand, or another soft substance, making them three dimensional. Casts can be made of these impressions by pouring casting material into the print and wait-ing for it to harden. The result is a precise, life-sized copy of the object that made the print. Casts can capture uneven surfaces of an impression, such as a shoe or tire on which one side has been worn down more than the other side. If the impression is deep enough, a cast can even make a record of the outer and inner edges of a shoe or tire. Casts provide solid, touchable evidence that is difficult to argue against in court. "Being able to match a shoe, a chisel, or a tire to its cast resonates with jurists," says Genge. "There's no question about scale, or fudged photographs, or biased interpretation of any kind."[32]

Until recently, plaster of Paris was the material most often used to create casts of impressions at crime scenes. However, investigators have found that dental stone, the substance den-tists use to make casts of their patients' teeth, creates stronger casts than plaster of Paris. Dental stone casts do not erode, even if they are cleaned to remove dirt so that details such as the brand label imprinted on the sole of a shoe can be read. For that reason, dental stone has become the substance of choice for most crime scene experts who make casts of impressions.

Not all impression evidence is left in soft substances, however. As with fingerprints, many impressions are left on hard surfaces such as floors or door jambs. These are two-dimensional and cannot be preserved by casting. Instead, they must be photo-graphed and then lifted, in a similar way to fingerprints.

A forensic scientist compares the cast of a shoe made from a crime scene with a possible match. Casts provide solid, touchable evidence that is difficult to argue against in court.

Fuming Techniques

Investigators have limited time and resources, and they often must put more effort into collecting fingerprints than impressions. Still, there are various methods for lifting an impression from a flat surface, and a few techniques used to develop fingerprints have also been used on footwear and other impressions. Crime scientists have been known to use cyanoacrylate (superglue) fuming to develop and enhance footwear impressions, especially those with traces of mud or dried water marks on them. Scientists have discovered that superglue fuming works on latent fingerprints because the fumes stick to liquid, and latent prints are about 98 percent water. The superglue technique also works for shoe prints left in dried liquid because the glue fumes stick to and condense on the moisture. This makes superglue fuming as useful for developing certain footwear impressions as it is for fingerprints. "If footwear impressions are composed of dried liquid, cyanoacrylate fuming may be the best method to use for impression development and enhancement," say P. E. Llewellyn, Jr., and L. S. Jenkins in a footwear impressions article titled "New Use for an Old Friend."[33]

Dust Tracks

Impressions, especially footprints, are often found in dry dust on a surface or a floor. These impressions can be as important for solving crimes as the three-dimensional prints left in mud or snow. But dust impressions are often hard to find and even more difficult to collect. They can also be easily destroyed by investigators moving through a crime scene in search of other types of evidence. "It is imperative that first responders and crime scene technicians be aware of the possibility that dust impressions, and the transferring of the dust from shoes to surface, exist at crime scenes," says Jan LeMay in her article "Evidence beneath Your Feet: Electrostatic Dust Lifting Collects Hidden Evidence at the Crime Scene." According to LeMay, if dust impressions exist at the scene of a crime, the investigators on duty "must make every effort, through available technology, to preserve, document, and collect it."[34]

Tracks or prints found in dust are one of the most difficult types of evidence to collect since they can be so easily destroyed.

Unlike a fingerprint, which can be dusted with powder and lifted with a small strip of tape, a footprint in dust cannot be powdered. It also cannot be cast. Static electricity is the key to collecting this kind of evidence.

Static Grabs Dust

Static electricity is an electrical charge created when two items are slid against each other so that they become electrically attracted to one another. A balloon rubbed against a head of hair makes the hair appear to "stick" to the balloon. This is static electricity in action.

In the 1960s, crime scene investigators facing the problem of gathering dust from a shoe print came up with the idea to rub a sheet of celluloid with a woolen cloth, creating static electricity. The celluloid, waved over the dusty imprint, lifted the dust particles, which stuck to the celluloid sheet directly and clearly in the exact formation of the shoe print.

Modern technologists have taken this simple technique a step further with the invention of electrostatic print lifters (ESPLs). These use a high-voltage current of electricity and a disposable lifting film to collect impressions left in dust particles. ESPLs can collect dusty shoe impressions not just from smooth nonporous surfaces but also from porous surfaces such as couch cushions, and even from human skin.

Impressions collected on ESPL film are very fragile and must be photographed right away. In spite of the extra care that investigators must take with them, Bodziak says they are invaluable to modern-day evidence collection. "The ability to electrostatically lift dry origin impressions is one of the most significant contributions to the scientific detection and recovery of footwear impression evidence at crime scenes," Bodziak says, adding that the technology is "relatively inexpensive and enables the recovery of highly detailed footwear impressions that otherwise could not be detected or recovered."[35]

From tooth marks to tire tracks, finding and preserving impressions can be as important to crime scene analysis as looking for fingerprints. Impressions not only provide a wealth of possible evidence to capture and charge criminals, they can help tell the story of what really happened at the crime scene. Few criminals bother to cover their tracks, so an expert with a good eye for detail can often find marks and imprints that could be the key to solving a crime.

CHAPTER 5

Fingerprints, Past and Future

For as long as police officers have used fingerprints to solve crimes, criminals have been thinking up ways to hide them. They have carved, sliced, sanded, scraped, and burned their fingertips to destroy the telltale markers. Some criminals have even had secret operations to have their fingerprints surgically changed.

Such self-mutilation was particularly popular in the 1930s, when fingerprint science was becoming more effective at catching crooks and when the gangster era was in full swing, giving police plenty of criminals to catch. The infamous gangster John Dillinger attempted to destroy his prints by dipping his fingertips in corrosive acid. This agonizing procedure gave him little benefit. He was shot to death even before he could pay for his crimes in prison. But when his fingerprints were taken at the morgue and compared to the ones police had recorded during a previous arrest, the two sets identified the same man. Had he been captured, his acidified fingers would still have betrayed him.

Dillinger was certainly not the only criminal to mutilate his hands. In 1953, police in Denver, Colorado, arrested a man who had performed his own crude skin grafts, slicing off his fingertips and laying them upside-down on different fingers. He bandaged them until the grafts took hold. But the tedious and painful process preserved all the ridge details of the original fingerprints. A clever examiner would merely have had to turn the impression evidence upside down to make a match.

Still other criminals go to such great lengths to destroy their fingerprints that they actually make their fingertips stand out more to investigators. A jagged scar running through a fingerprint, for example, leaves its own unique impression throughout a crime scene. If the criminal is a repeat offender, investigators will instantly know they have seen that scarred print before.

Such was the case for a felon named Roscoe Pitts. He mentioned, in an interview from his South Carolina prison cell in 1958, that any policeman in America could spot his prints from across a room. "Any crook who has his fingerprints rubbed off is nuts," he said. "If I had fingerprints, I probably wouldn't be behind bars today. It's given me nothing but grief."[36]

In an attempt to avoid capture, the 1930s gangster John Dillinger tried to destroy his own fingerprints by dipping his fingers in acid.

Hiding Prints

The fate of men like John Dillinger and Roscoe Pitts seems to have taken the glamour out of removing one's fingerprints. Modern criminals who wish to avoid fingerprint identification are more likely to wear gloves while they do their dirty work. Movies and TV shows also portray smart criminals who have mastered the technique of "wiping down" cars or other areas to get rid of their prints. But real-life latent print examiners are no less cunning. They have developed methods to lift prints from inside gloves, for example. And even if one print has been forgotten inside a vehicle, techniques such as superglue fuming can literally make it glow.

TV shows also ignore the fact that real-life criminals are not acting from scripts. They are generally nervous, jumpy, and eager to put distance between themselves and their crimes. It is quite likely that they will forget to clean up some of their footprints or fingerprints or skip the attempt altogether as they flee from the scene.

Can Fingerprints Be Dated?

In 1984, a realtor found the bodies of a Hispanic woman and toddler on a piece of agricultural property. Close to the bodies, investigators found two aluminum beer cans and determined the cans had spent eight hours in the sun. The day after the murder, the woman's boyfriend was questioned and admitted to sharing beer and fried chicken with his girlfriend and her daughter—but he said this had happened a week earlier, not the night before. A print on one of the cans matched the boyfriend's right thumb, and latent print specialists determined that a fingerprint on an aluminum can would not show such clear detail after spending a week in the sun. The boyfriend was convicted for both murders.

This is why latent-print and impression experts and are called in to almost every crime scene. Impression evidence has a long-standing history of successfully catching and convicting criminals. Old as the practice may be, modern technology is constantly finding new and better ways to locate fingerprints and other impressions and use them to solve crimes.

New Uses for Fingerprints

Advances in fingerprint technology have made this crime science useful for solving a variety of crimes. The fairly recent breakthrough of lifting fingerprints from plastic bags, for example, has brought fingerprint experts to the forefront of the war on drugs. More than 90 percent of the evidence examined at the U.S. Drug Enforcement Administration's South Central Laboratory in Texas takes the form of plastic bags or other plastic containers. Using cutting-edge techniques such as vacuum metal deposition, latent print examiners can now lift evidence from these bags that helps to identify drug offenders and bring them to justice.

Faster and more efficient fingerprint databases have also put latent print experts in the middle of the war on terrorism. Forensic specialists are being sent overseas to collect fingerprints in places that have been occupied by suspected terrorists such as members of Al Qaeda. These prints are then fed into a database in the hope of matching them with the name of a known terrorist.

The Department of Homeland Security (DHS) now maintains a database of the fingerprints of every non-citizen coming into the United States. By linking this database with the one maintained by the FBI, the U.S. government can quickly identify whether a known overseas criminal or a repeat violator of immigration laws is trying to get into the country.

> **By the Numbers**
>
> **340:**
> **Number of World Trade Center victims who were identified by their fingerprints after the 9/11 terrorist attacks**

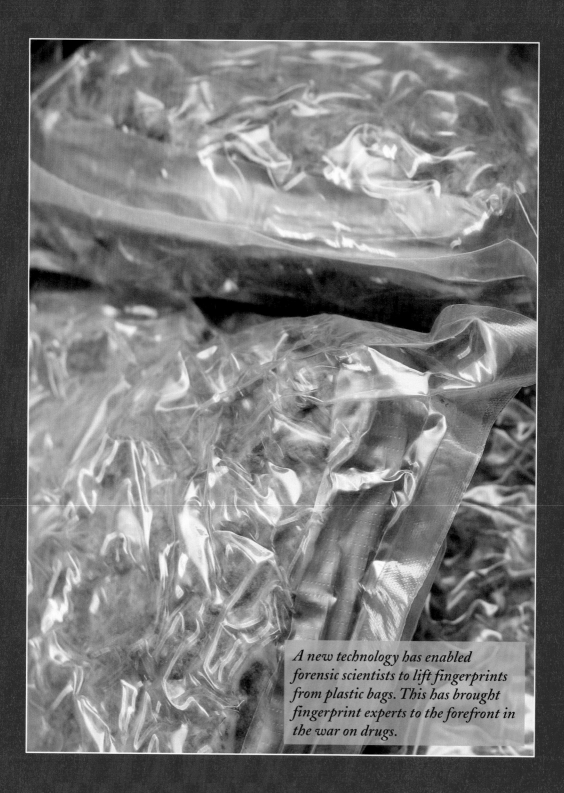

A new technology has enabled forensic scientists to lift fingerprints from plastic bags. This has brought fingerprint experts to the forefront in the war on drugs.

License to Fingerprint

In 2005, the U.S. Congress passed the Real ID Act. It asks the Department of Homeland Security to develop a standard driver's license and identification card to be used by all fifty states. The ID cards will probably include a biometric identifier, and the likely choice is a fingerprint.

This registered traveler card carries fingerprint information. It is similar to the standard driver's license proposed by the Real ID Act.

Thousands of people have been turned away at the border for this reason. Security will get even tighter as the DHS upgrades its system to capture all ten of a foreign visitor's fingerprints, instead of just the first two. "In effect, it requires foreign visitors to submit to the kind of extensive fingerprinting usually reserved for criminals," says Warren Richey, staff writer for *The Christian Science Monitor*. "But officials say that collecting all ten prints ensures compatibility with the FBI database, and increases the investigative utility of the computerized system."[37]

The fingerprint database can also identify a match between an incomer's fingerprints and one that was collected from a known terrorist location. This gives the government an invaluable early-warning system that a potential terrorist has crossed the border.

The Future of Fingerprints

In the last century, lawful citizens have benefited from knowing that the standard practice of fingerprint evidence can catch criminals and set innocent suspects free. Fewer crimes go unsolved, because fingerprints can be used to pull one particular name and identity out of a database of millions. Juries faced with proving the guilt or innocence of a suspect feel more comfortable with their decision when they are able to base it on evidence as strong as a fingerprint.

Fingerprints for Security

Honest citizens benefit from fingerprint technology in other and ever-increasing ways. For example, personal scanning systems have been developed to replace standard key locks for doors to private homes and businesses. Rather than fumbling for keys, a person can simply press a finger to the scanning device, and the door will open. The advantages of such a system are many. Criminals cannot pick these locks. The nuisance of a lost key becomes a thing of the past. Families no longer need to worry about finding sneaky places to hide spare keys. And new fingerprints can easily be added or deleted from the system's memory,

Fingerprints are now being used in personal scanning systems. For example, at this hotel in Monaco guests use their fingerprints, instead of keys, to enter their rooms.

so it is no longer necessary to have extra keys made or to change the locks on a house if a key gets lost or stolen.

Similar technology is being developed to replace password-sensitive devices such as personal computers and cell phones. The need to memorize different passwords and pin numbers may one day disappear. A simple scan of a finger will give quick access to portable devices. And unlike a password, a fingerprint pattern cannot be guessed—if an item such as a cell phone is lost, it cannot be used by anyone whose fingerprint does not match the owner's.

If fingerprint scanning one day becomes as common as passwords and keys, however, criminals may find ways to fool the new technology. Fingerprint scanning equipment may not be able to tell the difference between a real fingerprint and a photograph or a mold that has been made of the fingerprint, for example. And the scanning technology raises the troubling possibility that a determined criminal may find a way past the scanning system, even if it requires removing the required finger from its owner's hand.

Heat-sensitive scanning devices may offer one solution for problems like these. A person would only be admitted by providing a *warm* fingerprint. It is also possible that fingerprint scanning technology will be combined with passwords to help keep the wrong people from entering a building or accessing bank account information.

Because of their many advantages, fingerprint identification systems are becoming more common in school districts, hospitals, day care centers, and other locations where people may be volunteering, applying for work, or stopping by to visit or pick up a loved one. A fingerprint scan on a portable unit can quickly perform a background check by running through a database and looking for matches to known local criminals. Using a workstation with a fingerprint-reading device that is about the size of a palm pilot, the hospital, school, or day care center performs a rapid database search. If a convicted felon or other person known to be dangerous is trying to apply for work or gain access to a child or a hospital patient, the institution is quickly made aware.

Fingerprints can also help safeguard people who are memory impaired. The fingerprints of people who have Alzheimer's disease or other forms of dementia can be stored in a database in case a patient wanders away from home and gets lost. Using the fingerprint system, police can quickly identify who the elder is and take him or her back home. For caretakers of the elderly, this technology will provide tremendous peace of mind.

By the Numbers

1 IN 4:

Proportion of Americans whose fingerprints are on file with the FBI

Scientists are always finding new ideas and uses for fingerprints. In some cities, for example, fingerprint technology is being used on voting days to prevent anyone from trying to cast a ballot twice. In the years to come, it may be hard to picture life without fingerprint technology.

Setting the Standard in Fighting Crime

Fingerprint and impression evidence is not the newest thing in police work. In the 1890s, American novelist Mark Twain wrote a story about a detective who used fingerprints to solve a crime. Ever since then, the idea of catching crooks by the prints they leave at crime scenes has been one of the most popular themes in mystery novels, movies, and TV shows, to say nothing of the countless true-life cases that have been solved because of a fingerprint or a footprint.

Impression evidence has made a mark on the way we think about solving crime. In spite of its age, it remains one of the most traditional, reliable, and proven methods at the disposal of crime-scene experts. Scientists never stop looking for new ways to solve crimes—both new crimes and old, unsolved crimes—using this kind of evidence.

This photo shows a fingerprint which anthropologists believe is that of artist Leonardo da Vinci.

In 2006, anthropologists reconstructed what they believe to be a complete print of artist Leonardo da Vinci's left index finger. They used photographs of about two hundred partial fingerprints left on papers da Vinci handled during his life hundreds of years ago. And scientists are still studying letters written by the notorious nineteenth-century slayer Jack the Ripper during his bloody killing spree, probably the most famous unsolved serial murder case of all time. One of the Ripper's letters bears two of his fingerprints, left clearly (and perhaps on purpose) in red ink. But because Scotland Yard was just beginning to use fingerprints as a crime-fighting tool at the time and no real database of fingerprints was kept in Jack the Ripper's day, the fingerprints will probably never be enough to learn who this vicious killer really was.

Impressions may be an old form of evidence, but they are far from becoming outdated. Science is continually finding new ways to process this evidence, making it more and more difficult for crooks to get away with their crimes. And because impressions, particularly fingerprints, have been stored and studied for so many years, the new techniques and methods make it possible to revisit some unsolved cases that are decades old and find answers using modern science. "The durability of a latent print is variable," says Evans, "but if it is made on a hard, protected surface and left untouched, it is virtually permanent. Latent prints have been found and developed from objects in ancient tombs."[38]

Impressions evidence is clearly here to stay. "It is the lowest cost forensic crime-fighting tool in the arsenal of the investigator," says Ford.

A great detection tool for volume vehicle and burglary crime, border control, and also for the major crimes of homicide and terrorism, it will continue to solve more crimes per year than any other forensic detection and identification process.[39]

Notes

Introduction: A Criminal's Touch

1. Personal interview, Gary W. Jones, former supervisory fingerprint specialist for the FBI, April 25, 2007.

Chapter One: Identity by Fingers

2. Gaye Shahan, "Heredity in Fingerprints," *Identification News* April: 9–15, (1970), p. 14.

3. Colin Beavan, *Fingerprints: The Origins of Crime Detection and the Murder Case That Launched Forensic Science*. New York: Hyperion, 2001, p. 14.

4. Tom Harris, "How Fingerprint Scanners Work," How Stuff Works, 2007 http://computer.howstuffworks.com/fingerprint-scanner.htm.

5. N. E. Genge, *The Forensic Casebook: The Science of Crime Scene Investigation*. New York: Ballantine, 2002, p. 44.

6. Genge, *Forensic Casebook*, p. 21.

7. Genge, *Forensic Casebook*, p. 21.

8. Simon Cole, *Suspect Identities: A History of Fingerprints and Criminal Identification*.

Cambridge, MA: Harvard University Press, 2001.

Chapter Two: The Search for Hidden Prints

9. Quoted in Connie Fletcher, *Every Contact Leaves a Trace*. New York: St. Martin's Press, 2006, p. 16.

10. Fletcher, *Every Contact*, p. 15.

11. Personal interview, Allyn DiMeo, forensic specialist, May 14, 2007.

12. DiMeo, personal interview.

13. Personal interview, Graham Ford, certified latent print examiner, May 13, 2007.

14. Ford, personal interview.

15. Genge, *Forensic Casebook*, p. 179.

16. Quoted in Fletcher, *Every Contact*, p. 43.

Chapter Three: Making an Identification

17. Genge, *Forensic Casebook*, p. 40.

18. Cole, *Suspect Identities*, p. 89.

19. Joe Nickell and John F. Fischer, *Crime Science: Methods of Forensic Detection* Lexington, KY: University Press of Kentucky, 1999, p. 116.

20. Jones, personal interview.

21. Harris, "How Fingerprint Scanners Work".

22. Harris, "How Fingerprint Scanners Work"

23. Genge, *Forensic Casebook*, p. 43.

24. Beavan, *Fingerprints*, p. 11.

25. Douglas Ubelaker and Henry Scammell, *Bones: A Forensic Detective's Casebook* New York: Edward Burlingame, 1992, p. 66.

26. Genge, *Forensic Casebook*, p. 42.

Chapter Four: Impressions

27. Genge, *Forensic Casebook*, p. 67.

28. Quoted in Sina Najafi and Frances Richard, "The Sole of the Criminal: An Interview with William Bodziak," *Cabinet Magazine Online* Fall (2002) www.cabinetmagazine.org/issues/8/soleofthecriminal.php

29. Dwayne S. Hilderbrand, "Footwear: The Missed Evidence," Crime Scene Investigator, 2007, www.crime-scene-investigator.net/footwear.html

30. Nickell and Fischer, *Crime Science*, p. 148.

31. Ford, personal interview

32. Genge *Forensic Casebook*, p. 62.

33. P. E. Llewellyn, Jr., and L. S. Dinkins, "New Use for an Old Friend," *Journal of Forensic Identification* 45(5): 498—503 (1995), p. 498.

34. Jan LeMay, "Evidence beneath Your Feet: Electrostatic Dust Lifting Collects Hidden Evidence at the Crime Scene," *Law Enforcement Technology* 33 (3): 42, 44, 46, 48 (2006); p. 42.

35. William Bodziak, "Shoe and Tire Impression Evidence," *FBI Law Enforcement Bulletin* 53 (7): 2–12 (1984), p. 2.

Chapter Five: Fingerprints, Past and Future

36. Quoted in Moenssens, *Fingerprint Techniques.* Radnor, PA: Chilton Book Company, 1971, p. 58.

37. Warren Richey, "US Creates Terrorist *Fingerprint Database,*" *The Christian Science Monitor,* December 27, 2006, www.csmonitor.com/2006/1227/p01s03-usfp.html.

38. Colin Evans, *The Casebook of Forensic Detection: How Science Solved 100 of the World's Most Baffling Crimes.* New York: John Wiley & Sons, 1996, p. 92.

39. Ford, personal interview

Glossary

arch: A type of fingerprint pattern in which the ridges form a hill or a tent.

Automated Fingerprint Identification System (AFIS): A computerized system for scanning, storing, and retrieving fingerprint records from a central database.

cyanoacrylate: A chemical compound more commonly known as Superglue.

dactyloscopy: The science of studying fingerprint patterns.

dental stone: A durable substance used by dentists to create casts of their patients' teeth; it is also used to make casts of impression evidence.

DFO: Short for a chemical called 1,8-diazafluoreneone, which can develop prints on paper that are visible only with a specialized light source.

electrostatic print lifter (ESPL): A device that uses an electrical current and a disposable film to collect dust impressions at a crime scene.

fluoresce: To give off light; glow.

friction skin: Skin on the soles of the feet and the palms of the hands that is ridged for gripping things.

fuming: A technique in which an object to be fingerprinted is exposed to vapors of a substance that react with the print to make its pattern visible.

hit: A possible fingerprint match produced by a computerized fingerprint database.

Information-Based Identification System (IBIS): A portable, hand-held device police officers can carry with them to scan fingerprints of suspected criminals and do background checks on the spot.

lampblack: Standard black powder used to develop fingerprints on nonporous, light-colored surfaces.

latent: Hidden or hard to see.

loop: A type of fingerprint pattern in which the ridges double back on themselves.

magna brush: A magnetic wand that collects metallic powder to be lightly dusted over fingerprints.

minutiae: Tiny details in fingerprint patterns, such as forks and merges in the ridges; used to make fingerprint comparisons.

ninhydrin: A chemical that reacts with amino acids in human sweat to turn latent prints purple; it is known for causing headaches.

overdeveloping: Applying too much of a powder or chemical treatment to a print, thus ruining it.

papillary ridges: Tiny furrows in friction skin that create traction for gripping and form in patterns that are unique to every individual.

patent: Clearly visible.

plaster of Paris: A quick-setting, calcium-based mixture used to create molds of impressions.

plastic: A three-dimensional impression that has been set into a soft substance.

porous: Having pores; a surface that can soak up water or fingerprint powder.

silver nitrate: A chemical used for developing fingerprints, especially on paper.

sticky-slide powder: A substance that helps to develop fingerprints left on sticky items such as adhesive tape.

sudan black: A chemical that develops fingerprints on oily surfaces.

vacuum metal deposition (VMD): The process of coating a fingerprint with a thin layer of gold and zinc inside a vacuum chamber.

whorl: A type of fingerprint pattern in which the ridges form circles around a central point.

For More Information

Books

Colin Beavan, *Fingerprints: The Origins of Crime Detection and the Murder Case That Launched Forensic Science*. New York: Hyperion, 2001. A chronological look at the history and development of fingerprint science since the 1905 double murder in Britain that pioneered the use of this forensic technique. Chapters feature milestones in fingerprint methodology through the years.

William J. Bodziak, *Footwear Impression Evidence: Detection, Recovery, and Examination*, 2nd edition. Boca Raton, FL: CRC Press, 2000. A comprehensive look at the recovery of footprint evidence at crime scenes. Includes sections on casting, lifting, and photographing foot impressions.

Colin Evans, *The Casebook of Forensic Detection: How Science Solved 100 of the World's Most Baffling Crimes*. New York: John Wiley & Sons, 1996. Explains the science and reasoning detectives used to solve famous crimes. Each case includes a short paragraph about its forensic significance. Includes sections on fingerprinting and trace evidence.

Connie Fletcher, *Every Contact Leaves a Trace*. New York: St. Martin's Press, 2006. A collection of excerpts from personal interviews with forensic investigators and crime scene specialists. Fascinating, first-person accounts of the details, both mundane and extraordinary, that compose this line of work.

Federal Bureau of Investigation, *The Science of Fingerprints*. New York: Skyhorse Publishing, 2007. The FBI's own handbook on the subject, this work presents historical and modern fingerprinting techniques, explores the problems of the science, and explains how fingerprints are collected and filed, all supported with photographs and charts.

David Owen, *Hidden Evidence: Forty True Crimes and How Science Helped Solve Them*. Buffalo, NY: Firefly Books, 2000. O. J. Simpson, Jack the Ripper, the kidnapping of the Lindbergh baby, and the Kennedy assassination are among the famous crimes analyzed. A chapter is devoted to fingerprints and shoeprints.

Web sites

Court TV (www.courttv.com). The interactive Virtual Forensic Lab gives information on bite marks, fingerprints, shoeprint comparisons, and more. Go to http://www.courttv.com/onair/shows/forensicfiles/techniques/print.html and click on the link "Forensic Lab." Also, practice making a thumbprint match at the online fingerprint game, http://www.courttv.com/forensics/game/thumbgame.html.

FBI Criminal Justice Information Services (http://www.fbi.gov/hq/cjisd/cjis.htm). Includes information on automated fingerprint identification systems, criminal background checks, how to take fingerprints, and a brief history of fingerprint science.

The South Carolina Criminal Justice Academy (www.sccja.org). "Casting Footwear Impression Evidence," http://www.sccja.org/csr-mix.htm, and "Plastic Bag Processed for Prints," http://www.sccja.org/csr-processing.htm, have step-by-step instructions and photographs of these evidence collection procedures.

The Thinkquest Library (http://library.thinkquest.org/04oct/00206/lo_i_experiments.htm#fing). Experiments are described for developing fingerprints using two techniques, iodine crystals and superglue fuming.

Periodicals

Peter Meyer, "FBI Crime Center," *National Geographic*, May 2005

"X Rays Detect Fingerprints," *Science News*, April 2, 2005

Internet Sources

Christine Craig and Jason Byrd, "How Does Fingerprint Powder Work?" Scientific American online, http://www.sciam.com/askexpert_question.cfm?articleID=000ADC70-F65E-

1D6B-90FB809EC5880000&sc=I100322

Kristi Essick, "Compaq to Launch Fingerprint ID Module for PCs," CNN.com, July 1, 1998, http://www.cnn.com/TECH/computing/9807/01/fingerprint.idg/

Brian Handwerk, "Born Without Fingerprints: Scientists Solve Mystery of Rare Disorder," National Geographic News, September 22, 2006, http://news.nationalgeographic.com/news/2006/09/060922-fingerprints.html

Phillip Jones, "Friction Ridges Make A Lasting Impression," Forensic Magazine, October/November, 2006, http://www.forensicmag.com/articles.asp?pid=114

Roland Jones, "Homeland Security Seen Spurring Biometrics: Big Government Contract Coming to Develop Fingerprint-ID System," MSNBC.com, January 20, 2004, http://www.msnbc.msn.com/id/3999879/

Agnieszka Lichanska, "Fingerprint Analysis," Encyclopedia of Espionage, Intelligence, and Security, 2004. http://findarticles.com/p/articles/mi_gx5211/is_2004/ai_n19126288

Katherine Ramsland, "Catching a Killer," Court TV Crime Library, http://www.crimelibrary.com/criminal_mind/forensics/fingerprints/1.html

Index

Picture Credits

About the Author

Jenny MacKay lives in Sparks, Nevada, with her husband, Andy, and their children, Ryan and Natalie. She is a science, technical, and medical editor and has written for many newspapers and magazines. Every week, she watches Forensic Fridays on Court TV.